D0350370

LIVING
FULLY

LIVING
FULLY

FINDING JOY IN EVERY BREATH

SHYALPA TENZIN RINPOCHE

New World Library
Novato, California

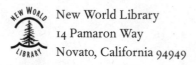 New World Library
14 Pamaron Way
Novato, California 94949

Copyright © 2012 by Shyalpa Tenzin Rinpoche

4766 7307 1/12

Text design by Tona Pearce Myers

Library of Congress Cataloging-in-Publication Data
Rinpoche, Shyalpa Tenzin, date.
Living fully : finding joy in every breath / Shyalpa Tenzin Rinpoche.
   p.   cm.
Includes index.
ISBN 978-1-60868-075-7 (hardcover : alk. paper)
1. Religious life—Buddhism. 2. Spiritual life—Buddhism. 3. Buddhism —Doctrines. I. Title.
BQ4302.R56 2012
294.3'444—dc23   2011040866

First printing, February 2012
ISBN 978-1-60868-075-7
Printed in Canada on 100% postconsumer-waste recycled paper

New World Library is a proud member of the Green Press Initiative.

10 9 8 7 6 5 4 3 2 1

To all my masters

Contents

Editor's Preface   xi
Introduction   I

CHAPTER ONE. *Living Fully*

Natural Freedom   9
Living Nakedly   II
The True Purpose of Being   13
Genuine Satisfaction   15

CHAPTER TWO. *The Intelligent Way to Begin*

The First Step   19
Kindhearted Intentions   21
Unlock the Chains of Self-Cherishing   23
A Daily Prayer   25
Innate Intelligence   27
The Spiritual Journey Is Our Journey   29

CHAPTER THREE. *The Qualities We Nurture*

Honesty   33
Sincerity   39
Respect   41
Generosity   43
Simplicity   45
Openness   47
Confidence   49

CHAPTER FOUR. *This Precious Moment*

Being Present in the Breath   53
Precious Human Birth   55
Cherish Life   59
Priceless Breath   61

CHAPTER FIVE. *Whatever Arises Ceases*

Embracing Change   65
The Supreme Meditation   69
Just a Short Stay   73

CHAPTER SIX. *Identity Crisis*

Territorial Self   77
Shattering Attachment   79
Free from the Notion of Self   81
Discovering the True Self   85

CHAPTER SEVEN. *Facing Obstacles and Obscurations*

Beyond Fixation   89
Look to the Source   91
Dissolving Emotional Afflictions   95
Conquering Your Enemies   101

CHAPTER EIGHT. *Sowing Seeds and Reaping Results*

The Unfailing Law of Karma   105
Going Around in Circles   109
Confronting Chaos   111
Fine-Tuning   113

CHAPTER NINE. *Perfect Freedom*

Free from Duality   117
Remember the Perfect Moment   119
Spontaneous Fulfillment   121
The Grass Isn't Greener   123

Nonattachment   125
Turn Toward Freedom   127
What Is Self-Liberation?   129
Not Clinging to Any Point of View   131

CHAPTER TEN. *Meditation as a Way of Life*

Meditation Is Necessary   135
Learning to Focus: A Basic Meditation   137
Practice All the Time   141
The Three Sublime Practices   143
Breathing Meditation: Hello and Goodbye   145
Nonmeditation Is the Ultimate Meditation   147

CHAPTER ELEVEN. *Practicing on the Path*

Nothing Is Working   151
This Is a Fantasy   155
To Follow the Buddha   159
Your Highest Standard   161
Coming and Going   163
Point Your Finger Inward   165
Accumulating Merit and Wisdom   169
A Savings Account for All Beings   171

CHAPTER TWELVE. *The Compassionate Heart*

The Four Boundless Qualities   175
A Pure Heart   181
Birth of the Compassionate Heart   183
The Profound Meaning of Compassion   185
Healing Self and Others   187
The Bodhisattva's Way   189

CHAPTER THIRTEEN. *The Essence of Mind*

The Hidden Jewel   193
Ocean of Wisdom   195

The Nature of Thought   197
Like a River   199
The Primordial Mirror   201

CHAPTER FOURTEEN. *Guidance of the Teacher*

Blessings of the Lineage   207
The Need for a Teacher   209
Respect and Appreciation   211
Unconditional Kindness of the Master   213
The Teacher Is Everywhere   217
Gesture of Devotion   219
Luminous Teacher   221

CHAPTER FIFTEEN. *Fearlessness*

Looking for Heaven   227
In the Face of Uncertainty   229
Look Inside the Fear   231
Fearlessness and the View   233

CHAPTER SIXTEEN. *Abundant Wealth*

Like a Small Flower   239
On an Island of Gold   241
Ceaseless Flow of Nectar   243
In the Presence of the Master   245
Understanding   247

Afterword: Questions about Love, Work, and Life
    with Shyalpa Rinpoche   249
Glossary   257
Index   263
About the Author   273
About Shyalpa Rinpoche's Centers and Projects   275

Editor's Preface

Living Fully: Finding Joy in Every Breath is a representative compilation of His Eminence Shyalpa Tenzin Rinpoche's spontaneous and profound teachings, imparted to his students in the United States for over two decades. Rinpoche's insights guide those who genuinely yearn to understand themselves and their world and to live a truly meaningful life. Just as a small key can open the door to the vast and splendid treasures hidden within a palatial mansion, these pithy and succinct teachings can reveal deep, penetrating, and life-changing instructions on how to transform and liberate one's mind.

The Bengali visionary, poet, and Nobel Prize–winner Rabindranath Tagore stated that "the object of education is freedom of mind, which can only be achieved through the path of freedom." This is precisely in accordance with how Rinpoche views the object of all spiritual practice and, indeed, the true purpose of our being. For Rinpoche, a fulfilling and meaningful life can only be enjoyed when genuine inner freedom is realized.

In the winter of 2007, His Eminence Shyalpa Tenzin Rinpoche suggested that his students publish a book of his teachings. The task of transcribing audio recordings of his talks had been underway for several years, so this appeared to be an auspicious time. Motivated by compassion and concern for the welfare of all, Rinpoche aspired to make the teachings on the sacred Buddhist path accessible to a broader audience.

As Saraha, the great Indian Buddhist master, said, "When the words of the teacher enter your heart, it is like holding a jewel in the palm of your hand." The task of mining these priceless jewels from Rinpoche's vast and profound treasury of teachings was daunting, but the work proved to be truly enriching. We are now pleased to present this inspiring and illuminating collection of precious teachings and instructions.

Living Fully: Finding Joy in Every Breath follows a loosely structured thematic progression. The reader can approach each chapter sequentially and allow time for reflection before continuing. The image of a spiral staircase is helpful in illustrating how central themes resurface organically with increasingly deeper meaning. The sections within each chapter may also be read independently if the reader feels that the topics address an immediate interest or concern. Each section is a complete teaching in and of itself. Although no written text can ever convey the power of an oral presentation, this format seemed to best represent Shyalpa Tenzin Rinpoche's spontaneous teaching style. Attentive and open-minded readers may uncover the profound subtext of his teachings, capable of piercing through to one's innate wisdom-nature. We encourage the reader to cherish this book as a trusted companion and use it as an effective guidebook for living fully.

Chapters 1 and 2 discuss the right attitude and approach with which to begin one's spiritual journey. Chapter 3 describes the qualities that are revealed and perfected along the way. Chapters 4 through 9 present teachings that shape the Buddhist path. Chapters 10 through 13 give guidance and instructions for one's personal journey. Chapters 14 and 15 discuss the role of the genuine teacher and the importance of relating to such a spiritual friend in order to live fearlessly and freely. Chapter 16 reaffirms the promise of the spiritual journey and encourages us to use our life well and live each moment fully. The text frequently mentions "our tradition," which can refer generally to the teachings of the Buddha or more specifically to the Buddhist tradition of the Great Perfection.

First and foremost, we would like to express our deepest gratitude to our kind root teacher, His Eminence Shyalpa Tenzin Rinpoche, for giving us the opportunity to immerse ourselves in these transformative teachings. Rinpoche demonstrated unwavering confidence in our capability and offered us continual inspiration, guidance, and support. Our foremost concern was that we not distort the meaning or intent of Rinpoche's message in preparing a manuscript for publication. Any errors or misrepresentations are solely our own.

After we completed a first draft of the manuscript, Rinpoche assisted us in organizing the contents in a clear and coherent manner. On numerous occasions, Rinpoche offered additional teachings and instructions where clarification or amplification was needed. This unique process of collaboration over a period of many years is testimony to Rinpoche's dedication to this project and his rapport with his students.

Many of Rinpoche's students contributed their time and talents in reviewing, selecting, organizing, and editing transcripts. Among these, we extend gratitude to Rich Reilly, Zach Larson, Sam Fohr, Carol Oberbrunner, Margaret LaFrance, Madalyn Smith, Marilyn Privett, Martha Donovan, Ives Waldo, George Saunders, Craig Davis, Cheryl Ramsdell-Speich, Emily Shuldman, and Louise Koval. There were many other students and friends of Rinpoche, too numerous to name here, who generously offered their advice and encouragement. The transcripts that Pema Tara produced from audio files were indispensable. Special thanks go to journalist, writer, and editor Deena Guzder for her invaluable editing and input.

We extend thanks to Jason Gardner, senior editor at New World Library, to copyeditor Jeff Campbell, and to our literary agent, Joy Azmitia of Russell & Volkening.

With this rewarding task completed, we dedicate the fruits of our labors with heartfelt joy, and pray that the words of our precious teacher will benefit countless beings.

Paul J. Patrick
Editorial Director,
Rangrig Yeshe

INTRODUCTION

The most amazing and sublime beings excel in living fully and never seem to dwell in the past. I witnessed this in my own great teacher, who after repeated requests wrote just three beautiful lines to summarize his life. On the other hand, some extraordinary masters wrote their life stories at length, and they are equally inspiring to read. The events of my own life are not so noteworthy, and I feel the message is far more important than the messenger. However, I was asked to give a brief recounting, so that I might create an auspicious and personal connection with interested readers.

I was born in the foothills of the majestic Himalaya Mountains. After my first birthday, my family moved to Orissa, in eastern India. While living in Tibet, my parents were well-to-do landowners, but after going into exile, they had to toil in the sun for long hours, felling trees and clearing land for their corn harvests. During my early childhood, my grandparents were primarily responsible for my care, and they nurtured me with affectionate love and concern. In a sense, they were my first teachers, as I learned from them how to protect and care for others.

Apparently, at an early age there were indications of the course my life was to take. My grandmother told me how, at age two, I would place my hands together in reverence upon entering the local temple. A senior reincarnate Buddhist lama from the area told my grandmother that I was destined to become a spiritual guide.

When I was four years old, I joined my father at the crack of dawn while he performed his daily rituals and prayers. I did not often play with toys like other children, but was more interested in spiritual objects like bells and drums. These sacred instruments forged my early connection to the teachings of the Buddha and initiated my lifelong spiritual journey.

At the age of six, I began to attend a public school for a secular education, and after returning home in the afternoon, I studied and memorized Buddhist scriptures until dinnertime. I would often hear my friends laughing outdoors while playing games of hide-and-seek and soccer. I longed to join them in the afternoon sun. However, my wise grandmother gently encouraged me to concentrate on my religious studies, believing in my destiny to become a spiritual leader.

On my fifteenth birthday, my grandfather asked me to choose a young girl from our village as my wife. However, at this young age I was more interested in continuing my studies, and I was accepted to the Central Institute of Higher Tibetan Studies in Sarnath, India. Each morning, my classmates and I learned ancient philosophy, rituals, and prayers. In the afternoon, we sat in the fragrant gardens surrounding the university and engaged in animated philosophical debate and discussion. With each passing year, my understanding of and faith in the spiritual way of life grew stronger.

During the sixth year of my studies, a letter arrived informing me that my grandfather had died. Deeply saddened, I returned home during the summer holidays, only to learn that my stepfather had also passed away and that both my parents were extremely ill. My mother was in a coma. I joined the monks and lamas in performing rituals for the dead and prayers for the sick. I concentrated on helping my parents regain their health, but their chances for recovery did not look promising.

In the Buddhist tradition, it is believed that rescuing animals that are destined for slaughter not only frees them from suffering but also creates favorable conditions for our long life. More importantly, expressing compassion in this way transforms negative obstacles for those who are near death. When you truly feel compassion in your heart, everything seems to go well. Spending most of the money that remained after paying medical bills, I ransomed the lives of thousands of fish and released them back into the River Ganges on the twelfth day of my mother's coma. Miraculously, my mother awoke and rested peacefully for the first time in weeks. Subsequently, my parents steadily regained their health.

After years of comprehensive study in the foundations of Buddhist philosophy, I met my root teacher and many other great masters from whom I received the teachings, transmissions, empowerments, and secret initiations of the Great Perfection tradition. The Great Perfection is the pinnacle of all Buddhist teachings, the ultimate path for achieving direct realization of the clear and lucid nature of the mind.

When I was twenty-one years old, I was invited to Kham, in eastern Tibet, to be instated as the spiritual leader of Shyalpa Monastery and Retreat Center. As part of my enthronement, the revered lama Khenpo Karma Dorje and other local lamas performed the Innermost Secret Puja of Padmasambhava. This ceremony offers prayers of aspiration to the Second Buddha, Padmasambhava, who brought the precious teachings of Buddhism from India to Tibet. I was humbled by their gracious reception. Their confidence in me strengthened my resolve to shoulder the responsibilities of guiding the monastery. It was an honor and privilege to serve in this way.

In 1987, I was invited to come to the United States to teach. I was intrigued about visiting there, as I had met many American tourists in Varanasi, India, who told me that their country was materially rich but spiritually impoverished. Arriving on the East Coast of the United States with only a hundred dollars in my pocket, I traveled across the country by road to Los Angeles and then back to Vermont, giving teachings along the way. I soon learned that many people in America were looking for instant gratification — whether it was fast food or quick enlightenment!

Some of my close students requested that I remain in America, and I lived for several years in the beautiful Berkshires of Massachusetts. I remained there in semi-retreat, studying and contemplating the *Seven Treasuries of Longchenpa,* the seminal work of one of Tibet's greatest scholars and meditation masters. My faith and trust in these profound teachings intensified, and I grew more determined to present these jewels of wisdom in a way that would be accessible to a growing audience of receptive seekers in the West.

In the years since, I have tried to fulfill the wishes of my teachers by sharing my understanding of Buddhist teachings and practices with spiritual aspirants around the world. I feel very blessed, having access to a wisdom tradition that can guide us toward complete fulfillment. We are so fortunate to have the time and interest to hear these teachings and put them into practice. Today, the teachings of the Buddha are still descending on us like a rain of sweet nectar. In this very lifetime, we are capable of awakening from the fog of our delusions and experiencing the radiant light of our true nature.

Those who continually experience the highest, richest qualities of their being are known as enlightened ones. The more we can integrate with the essential richness of our being, the more fully we can live. Then we can truly enjoy this precious life and celebrate each and every moment. Ultimately, there is no difference between the Buddha and ourselves. The Buddha actualized his enlightened qualities, and we too have the same potential.

The enlightened nature that exists within us is inherently perfect from beginningless time. We do not have to manufacture anything, since it is already perfect as it is. Our true nature shines like the sun. We need to always be aware of this unconditional luminosity, even on the darkest of days.

In this troubling age, when rigid ideologies and confusion often reign, the teachings of the Buddha beckon us home to the simplicity and freshness of our natural state. We do not need to concern ourselves with anything other than this fundamental state of being. Let us breathe freely, without all of the pressure and stress to which we have grown so accustomed. It is my heartfelt wish that these precious wisdom teachings will help to guide us straight to the essence of our true, unconditional nature. At peace with ourselves and at ease with the world, we can discover what it means to live each moment fully.

CHAPTER ONE

Living Fully

Natural Freedom

Whether we realize it or not, our deepest aspiration is to experience the richness and fullness of our being in every moment. Each of us has the capacity to live fully, but how do we recognize our potential? We usually think that the surest way to fulfillment is to satisfy our desires for the objects that bring us pleasure. However, when we grasp for pleasure in hopes of finding happiness, it will elude us. For instance, an ice cream sundae, a thrilling movie, or a glass of fine chardonnay can distort our natural quality. We may devour an entire chocolate bar when we feel lonely and unappreciated. Although we savor the taste of the chocolate and momentarily feel euphoric, the lonely, empty feeling soon returns. We do not experience the pure fulfillment inherent in every moment, and therefore, we tend to use sense pleasures as a temporary salve.

In the United States, we are proud of our freedoms and we frequently congratulate ourselves on the great liberties we enjoy. But it seems that we often do not make the best use of the leisure and opportunity that our freedom affords us. We tend to believe that free choice gives us the license to indulge. This may provide fleeting satisfaction. However, incessant pleasure-seeking is not the true way to enjoy our freedom.

When we know how to surrender, we can truly appreciate our freedom. The ability to surrender comes from a disciplined approach to life. In this case, surrender is not submitting to a higher authority, like an army recruit saluting a drill sergeant. Rather, we surrender when we give up trying to satisfy all of our hopes and expectations. If we can abandon our efforts to fabricate a "perfect" world, we will experience genuine freedom that is not corrupted by endless craving for something better. The more conviction we gain in our inner potential, the more willing we are to surrender in this natural way. We may begin to find pure pleasure in the most unexpected places.

Self-discipline provides us the space in which to surrender. It brings confidence in our inherent wealth. It is not about making stringent demands on oneself. Fasting and praying all day in a dark cave are not always necessary. Real discipline is not punishment; it is a peaceful path to insight and understanding. Lacking this kind of mental training, our habitual thinking gains the upper hand and imprisons us in our ordinary ways. Essentially, all of the myriad methods of spiritual practice are nothing but tools that help us leap beyond ourselves. With training, we can develop these skills. When we practice mindfulness and sharpen our awareness, we will not become trapped in mind-numbing routines and narrow views. We will open up vast reservoirs of fresh, self-renewing energy. Then we can live fully in the vitality of every breath.

Protecting and defending our self-image drains us of this sacred energy. Striving to define and validate our identity precipitates anxiety and stress. When we know who we are, we will be content. In the movement of each breath, we will enjoy natural freedom. Our disciplined way of life will become relaxed and effortless, and we will appreciate how simple it is to experience inner peace and lasting happiness.

LIVING NAKEDLY

Our most pressing challenge is to live fully. Our lives will not be truly satisfying if we cannot live each moment deliberately and grasp the essence of our precious human nature. Temporarily we may enjoy good health and material comforts, but our lives are rushing by, like sand running through an hourglass. What's more, there is no guarantee that we will awaken from our sleep tomorrow morning!

With this in mind, I sincerely advise you to breathe fully right now! Live mindfully, as if there were no tomorrow. Even if others think that seizing each moment makes you a little crazy, it's all right to be crazy once in a while, as long as you are crazy in a good way. There is no reason to always follow the norm. After all, what is the norm? Who creates the norm? When you clearly understand the preciousness and impermanence of life, you will live in a way that is most beneficial and meaningful to you. You will not depend on others for validation.

You may have friends and family who love you. But remember that you came into this life naked and alone, and you will leave naked and alone. So why not live nakedly? Why not live without any cover, without any pretense? Living nakedly means living each moment in your original, fresh form. When you are familiar with your unconditional self and not limited by relative circumstances, you will see everything as perfect.

Life is not a rehearsal. Don't compromise when it comes to

living in the present. Don't compromise with your past or future, with right or wrong, with good or bad. With a self-centered perspective, our minds are agitated by the extremes of hope and fear. We hope that things will work out for our benefit or we fear that they will not. Living fully means living without compromise. Do not allow your thoughts, feelings, or emotions to corrupt you. Attempt to honestly confront all your neuroses and negativity. If it helps, retreat to a secluded place where you can practice the teachings of the enlightened ones and investigate the workings of your mind.

Those who follow the Buddhist tradition are referred to as *practitioners* because they do not simply accept the Buddha's teachings without question, but instead apply the teachings and test their veracity, like a goldsmith examining gold to ensure that it is genuine. A Buddhist practices by training his or her mind, much like an athlete trains the body to compete in a marathon. Consistent training will gradually free you from unwholesome thoughts and negative emotions. The quintessential practice is to skillfully liberate your confusion on the spot, no matter where you are or what you are doing. This is the best way to live and the true way to practice.

THE TRUE PURPOSE OF BEING

The spiritual journey enables us to discover our innate intelligence — the essence of our being. When we behold this inner radiance, suffering[1] and darkness will vanish from our lives. In this very moment, we have the opportunity to dispel our ignorance[2] and enjoy a truly wholesome way of living. When our obscurations[3] are purified, confusion will disappear. If being in this human form has any purpose, it is to make good use of our lives so that we never get trapped in dark and hopeless realms, with little opportunity to utilize our intelligence.

However, we must be clear on one crucial point: we are all capable of deceiving ourselves. If we have suffered in the past or are suffering now, it is not someone else's fault; it is our own doing. Thinking we are clever, we fool ourselves. The teachings of the Buddha show us how to utilize our basic intelligence and

---

1. *Dukkha* is the Sanskrit word that is most often translated as "suffering." In Buddhist teachings, suffering is understood in the broadest sense. It refers to any disturbance in the mind, from the subtlest feelings of anxiety and unease to the most extreme states of agony and despair.

2. Ignorance (Tib. *ma rigpa*) is a lack of knowing, a failure to recognize the empty and lucid nature of mind itself. Ignorance perceives the self and phenomena as existing substantially, independently, and self-sufficiently.

3. Obscurations veil the innate purity of mind. There are two kinds of obscuration, emotional and cognitive. Emotional obscurations are attachment, aversion, and ignorance. Cognitive obscurations are fixed concepts about the nature of things.

avoid self-deception. Even if you spend years in solitary retreat, recite millions of mantras, and emerge as a great philanthropist, you might still be deceiving yourself. These days, many practitioners of the spiritual path — both Westerners and Easterners — claim to have meditated for many years and believe they have experienced great realization. However, some do not seem to know why they are meditating or how their practice enhances their way of living. This is a sign they have not yet realized the true purpose of being.

It is our good fortune as human beings to have the intellectual capacity to understand the meaning of impermanence. We should always remember that this human life is as transient and unpredictable as a summer rain shower. It is uncertain when life will end, but it is absolutely certain that it will end. Therefore, we should urgently pursue a spiritual path that helps us to actualize our innate, enlightened qualities. Only then will we know complete contentment and feel certain that we have fulfilled our purpose in life. I believe this is the best way to tackle our daily problems and embody an authentic way of spiritual living.

Genuine Satisfaction

We often attempt to apply conventional thinking and methods to solve our problems and find satisfaction, but this approach never seems to provide us with a truly effective solution. Will this ever bring us closer to unconditional joy and freedom?

In the West, we are free to do whatever we want and purchase whatever we please if we have a few dollars in our pocket. We can accomplish almost anything if we are resourceful enough. But placing our trust in achievements that are contingent and ephemeral is like believing in the reality of a mirage. We may rely on conditional circumstances for fulfillment, but we will always be left feeling thirsty for more. Everything in the relative world is conditional. Everything is dependent on causes and conditions that lack stability and are constantly shifting.

We fool ourselves when we think that achieving conditional goals will promise us lasting satisfaction. But we tend to get ensnared in our clever schemes and unwittingly waste our precious time. We run around in circles and maneuver in limited and self-serving ways.

Please do not misunderstand — we should be free to do what we like. However, the most pressing issue is this: we need to liberate ourselves from self-centeredness by subduing our pride and arrogance. Like prisoners escaping from shackles, we need to break free from the confusion and negativity that torment us.

Then we will rediscover the beauty of our natural state of being, released from all burdens and limitations.

Our true nature is pure, all-pervasive awareness. This awareness has no form, yet it reflects and manifests all appearances. Our quest in life is to discover our true nature and bask in the freedom of the unconditional, beyond limitations. Then we will never forget that every moment we are spending a priceless gift — *our breath*. The inhalation and exhalation of our breath, moment by moment, is precious. Here, there is always fresh discovery and continual revelation. Here, there is genuine satisfaction. So let's not rely too heavily on anything external. Let us always remember what is ours from the very beginning: the capacity to breathe deeply and to live our lives fully.

CHAPTER TWO

The Intelligent Way to Begin

The First Step

Life is indeed a precious opportunity. If we aspire to live fully, it is important to be clear about our intentions. It is best to begin every activity by examining our motivation. When we set out on a journey, we usually have an objective in mind. Is the trip for business or pleasure? Are we traveling for a job interview or to visit friends? What are we hoping to accomplish? Do we expect to have a good time, or are we anxious about the trip?

Examining our motivation is meaningful because the purity of our intention sets the tone for everything that follows. In our tradition, we say that everything rests on the tip of a wish. The quality of our motivation will govern the course of our journey and determine its eventual outcome.

Perhaps your motivation for reading this book stems from your interest in learning how you can live a happier life. If you feel this way, you must sense that everyone yearns to suffer less and live more joyfully. Everyone wants to be happy! We will find more satisfaction in whatever we do when we begin with the sincere wish that we all find happiness together.

Although we have periods in our lives that are relatively happy, we are rarely free from stress or anxiety. Everyone is struggling; everyone suffers. In a very real sense, we are all victims of our agitating thoughts and emotions. We may feel sorry for ourselves, but it is helpful to remember that all human beings are in the same predicament. We are all traveling companions on a sometimes perilous and difficult journey. When we journey together toward the goal of mutual happiness, we can ease our burdens and the burdens of others.

Taking your first step in this sublime way, your life will be enriched, like a beautiful tapestry being carefully sewn together with golden threads. Tenderly embrace the whole universe and recognize everyone as your partner on the journey. We are all in the same boat, so we should care for everyone equally. Elevating our thinking in this way is not always easy, because we spend so much time looking out for ourselves. Training your mind to think more of others will broaden your vision and soften your heart. Taking your first step with a kind heart is the intelligent way to begin.

KINDHEARTED INTENTIONS

To live our lives fully, we need to do everything completely. Complete activity begins with a pure intention. In other words, give rise to a kind heart.

When our actions are not imbued with kindness, we will not achieve perfect results. When our activities do not emanate from a pure heart, we limit our potential. Our lives feel empty and devoid of meaning. On the other hand, if we act with the aim of serving others, our lives will be uplifted and each breath will feel like a wonderful gift. A positive attitude beautifies our lives, just as a precious jewel beautifies the person who wears it. In the Buddhist tradition, the metaphor of an elixir is used to illustrate the transformative power of the kind heart. A benevolent wish is like an elixir that transforms ordinary base metals into precious gold.

When our activities are not guided by pure intentions, we soon lose enthusiasm and interest. No matter how exciting a project may seem initially, it ends in disappointment. A selfish thought is not a pure thought. Therefore, from the beginning, strengthen your resolve, purify your intentions, and awaken a kind heart. Your actions will shine with virtue and integrity. You will never feel defeated or discouraged. You will have respect for yourself and for others, a respect that is rooted in the fundamental goodness within all of us.

Whatever you plan to do, begin by taking a moment to reflect before you act. Generate a pure thought and nurture it within your heart. Keep it always in your mind. Have the sincere wish that every interaction you have with others will be the cause for their happiness in this and future lives, and that ultimately it will lead others to the unsurpassed happiness of complete enlightenment.

UNLOCK THE CHAINS
OF SELF-CHERISHING

When our motivation is pure, we can accomplish everything easily, like an eagle soaring effortlessly on the wind.
When we lack the noble aspirations of a compassionate heart,
we will not achieve anything worthwhile in our spiritual practice, even if we sit in meditation day and night for over a hundred
years. What matters most is not what we do, but how we do it.

Put a drop of poison in a glass of milk and you would not
drink it. If you are motivated purely by selfish aims, the results
could be just as deadly. On the other hand, if you are sincerely
interested in relieving the suffering and pain of others, your life
will flourish.

A miserly person who hoards wealth and cares nothing for
others feels lonely and unloved. If we focus too much on our own
desires and interests, we limit our chances for happiness. Caring
about others is the way to hone our emotional intelligence. If we
start with the noble aspiration to be helpful to all of humanity,
our lives will be blessed with joy and graced with purpose. We
begin with the sublime intention to achieve enlightenment for the
benefit of all. As we say in our tradition, sublime in the beginning, sublime in the practice, and sublime at the conclusion.

A genuine spiritual path loosens the chains of self-cherishing,
the tightness in our hearts that narrows our vision and limits our

horizons. True compassion illuminates our lives and helps us to guide others, just as a lighthouse signals a safe path for ships lost at sea. Always appraise your intentions by asking yourself, "Is this kindhearted?" Make this your natural way of living.

A Daily Prayer

To fully realize your potential and achieve genuine freedom, have compassion and caring for everyone at all times. If you can free yourself from selfish thoughts and actions, you will enjoy a natural sense of ease and independence.

Success on the spiritual path is contingent on fostering a pure intention. If your heart is pure, your path will be pure. You will feel that your life is much too precious to waste, and you will not have time for even a single thoughtless comment. You will see sacredness in all things.

On the Buddhist path, engendering a heart of compassion is the essential practice. The instant you wake up each morning — before you sip your coffee, brush your teeth, or take a shower — pause and recite this simple prayer:

> *May I act with pure motivation.*
> *May I part from selfish ways.*
> *May I bring joy and happiness to others.*
> *May I free them from pain and sorrow.*
> *May I have a big and open heart*
> *That encompasses the whole world.*

The power of these positive aspirations will bring liveliness and purpose to your whole day. Before you begin work, meet with your colleagues, eat your lunch, or relax with your family, arouse the spirit of a generous heart. At night, before you go to bed, reflect on your day and rejoice in the good intentions you had for others. You will have a restful sleep and wake up feeling refreshed.

Innate Intelligence

For a moment, contemplate this axiom: *Everyone wants to be happy, and there is no one who is interested in suffering.* Essentially, all beings are the same in this respect, whether we view them as friends or enemies.

Using our intelligence, we can understand this universal truth without needing religious dogma to convince us. Common sense tells us that everyone wants to be free from suffering and enjoy nothing but happiness. We pursue happiness in various ways, some by accumulating fortunes, some by chasing pleasure and entertainment, some by exploring the liberating potential of a spiritual path. But can we succeed if we seek happiness only for ourselves? Pursuing happiness in this one-sided way can never ensure lasting fulfillment. Generating universal concern and caring for others is the intelligent approach that promises mutual fulfillment. As the saying goes, "Do well by doing good."

In pursuit of happiness, our actions are often counterproductive, and we end up harming ourselves and others. We may deceive a loved one, alienate a friend, or cheat a business partner. Although we share a common desire for happiness, we often pursue happiness in narrow and self-serving ways. If you gorge on your favorite food, it could make you sick, and you may never want to eat that food again. However, if you use your common sense, you will eat in moderation. Similarly, we can grow sick from disturbing emotions when we are consumed with self-centered agendas. Just as our bodies can teach us not to overeat, our innate intelligence can prevent us from acting selfishly. Understanding this, we will act with more care and sensitivity. The wish to benefit others is the perfect remedy for all afflictions and suffering. It is the best of all wishes, as it can overcome all harmful thoughts. Be inseparable from this wish and never forsake it.

THE SPIRITUAL JOURNEY
IS OUR JOURNEY

The heart of spiritual practice is intimately connected with conviction in our limitless potential as human beings. Consciously or unconsciously, the journey of our life is taking place. When we travel mindfully,[1] we truly experience our world as sacred.

Many of us are skeptical about becoming "spiritual people"; however, spirituality is not something strange or foreign to us. The majesty of a fully grown oak tree resides within a tiny acorn. Spirituality resides within us always, so we are never undeserving of its blessings. As our birthright, all breathing beings have the potential for unlimited growth and spiritual maturity. An enlightened being is a breathing being just like you!

This profound spiritual journey is our journey, and it can fulfill our deepest aspirations. The true purpose of living is to reach our full potential. We should never doubt for a moment that we are capable of spiritual awakening. Spiritual masters do not have a monopoly on compassion. On the contrary, each individual inherently possesses basic goodness and the capacity for love and kindness. To experience the utmost quality of our being is our natural birthright. We are on a lifelong spiritual journey to the heart of our ultimate essence, the state of complete enlightenment.

---

1. Mindfulness is paying attention and focusing clearly on the activities of body, speech, and mind.

CHAPTER THREE

The Qualities We Nurture

Honesty

In Buddhist practice, honesty is an essential virtue. You cannot be completely honest with others unless you are willing to take an honest look at yourself. When you are honest with yourself, you will understand how to be a gentle, kind, and caring person. Why is this the case? Let's begin by examining the conditional nature of the world around us.

All conditional phenomena are subject to change because they lack permanent components and characteristics. This includes the so-called self. From an unenlightened perspective, the ego or "self" is what we believe to exist as an unchanging, independent, and separate entity. The notion of self is merely imputed upon a ceaseless continuum of thoughts, feelings, and perceptions. A careful examination of the self reveals it to be only a mistaken mental construct. If we thoroughly investigate this self, we find that it is temporary and does not exist in any substantial way. Nevertheless, we have a hard time accepting this. The self is constantly attempting to proclaim a distinct identity, separate from the rest of the universe, like an unruly child who insists on being the center of attention. The egocentric self wants to declare its independence — to continually reinterpret or deny reality. In other words, the self has its own agenda.

The self appears to have ambition; it wants to upgrade and improve things. It sees the countryside and imagines a house. It builds a house but is not yet satisfied. The self begins to feel that the house is not good enough. It needs a walk-in closet just for shoes, a Sub-Zero refrigerator, and a six-car garage. The house is too close to the neighbor's house or too far from the lake. The rooms are too small. The kitchen is too dark. This desire to improve things arises in manifold ways, but at the heart of this desire there is always the absence of honesty.

Real honesty is seeing reality as it is and not struggling to change it. Of course, this is not so easy to do. It is counterintuitive. From the moment we are born, we are taught to divide the world into "me" and "everything else," and we are encouraged to pursue that which profits "me," leaving "everything else" to fend for itself.

What has this way of thinking brought us? This constant denial of reality takes great energy, but it is a losing battle that ends in failure. There is something unnatural about it. It cannot make us happy because reality is always refusing to cooperate, refusing to corroborate our beliefs about the division between self and others. When we finally achieve the things we desire, we fear losing them, and this triggers constant anxiety. There is a feeling of sadness and frustration born of our inability to make the world conform to our hopes and expectations. And at the time of our demise, we finally have to confront the lie of our ego and the truth of impermanence.

Honesty means living without fabrication, pretense, or foolishness. Honesty means living simply. The culmination of true honesty is a life that is free from frivolous preoccupations. As you simplify your life, you will not get hooked on external stimuli. You can be free and relaxed, like a skylark gliding on the wind.

True honesty also means experiencing each moment completely. When you are dishonest, you miss the present moment because you are lost in thoughts of the past or future. Therefore, you fail to enjoy the only moment that is complete. Not paying full attention to this moment, you fail to integrate with the energy of the present. When we ignore the present moment, there are consequences: we create karma and suffering. If we live in the moment only 50 percent of the time, the 50 percent we ignore will cause us difficulties later.

In this tradition, when we say "Be mindful" it implies that this moment is more profound than anything else on earth. Your innate nature is pure and perfect; therefore, the energy emerging from this essence has complete validity and every moment of your life is completely valid. Whether you are musing about your father, listening to a flock of geese flying overhead, or feeling irritated because tax time is approaching, each of these moments is nothing other than fresh energy emanating from the core of your being.

If, for example, you experience a moment of jealousy, do not disregard or hide from this jealous feeling. Be completely aware of your jealousy, with the understanding that jealousy is simply energy. This energy is every bit as much "you" as any other energy that has ever emanated from "you." Because this jealous energy is legitimate, you must respect it. You must not ignore it, theorize about it, or reject it. You must simply pay complete attention to it.

When you pay complete attention to it, the energy will not demand anything more. It will be complete because you have paid total attention. It will not ruin your day, or haunt you tomorrow. Having been experienced fully, energy will simply run its course.

The energy of jealousy is no different from the energy associated with the pleasure of eating, the stab of a pin, or the sound of music from a passing car. These are all expressions of pure energy in a ceaseless continuum. Fully experiencing this continuous display is the practice of true honesty.

Our thoughts and emotions are like a snake that has tied itself into a knot. If we respect the snake and recognize its amazing flexibility, we will have confidence in the snake's ability to untie itself. The most skillful way of being is to remain completely present in the moment with awareness. Then the snake will unravel itself naturally!

Dishonesty creates selfishness, preventing us from living fully. When we are not being honest with the reality of the present moment, we worry, "If I do this, what is in it for me? What will happen to me?" The "me" becomes more important than the moment, like static in a radio broadcast drowning out the message.

Letting the moment take over is the practice of true honesty. To let the moment take over, you must have great confidence in the Buddha within. When you find the Buddha within, everything becomes a celebration. You will see everything as an expression of your wakeful nature. Joy is an expression of the Buddha within. Sorrow is also an expression of the Buddha within. Everything is an expression of the Buddha within, so everything is your creation. Understanding reality in this way, there will be no reason for dishonesty. You will no longer feel the need to fight or the need to change. You will accept and embrace things just as they are.

One might wonder, "Does this condemn us to a life of passivity? If everything is perfect as it is, should we just sit on the couch and watch life go by?" Actually, this is not the case. Being honest simply means seeing things as they truly are. Therefore, our actions will be guided by clear seeing, and not based on delusions or wishful thinking. Our behavior, in turn, will be naturally honest.

Driving down the highway in summer, we see heat waves shimmering from the road's surface. Do these heat waves serve any useful purpose? They only obscure the real conditions ahead of us. These heat waves may be likened to dishonesty. As they dissipate, we see the road more clearly; we see all of its beauty and dangers. In the same way, as we become more honest, we experience life more fully. Seeing reality just as it is — not judging, categorizing, or trying to change it — we respond to life's demands more competently. We are open to the joy of life and the sadness of life. We are open to everything.

What is so intimidating about seeing things just as they are? What is really frightening is denying the truth, and no matter how much we deny, it will not change reality. When we refuse to acknowledge the truth, it is like leaping across a ravine with our eyes shut. We can deny all we like, but it will not change the nature of the ravine. We should open our eyes and face the situation just as it is. Then we can proceed with full knowledge of the conditions, and accept responsibility for the outcome.

Here we see the birth of complete intelligence, wisdom that frees us from the weight of all consequences. This is what is required to live fearlessly. We do not become fearless by believing that we will never experience conflict or harm. True fearlessness comes from the conviction that we will never lie to ourselves. We will never run and hide from a single moment of our lives. We will be fully present in every moment and accept every consequence.

At the beginning of our journey, this kind of honesty is partly willed. You should make an effort not to rationalize, not to delude yourself. Look frankly at each situation and consider the possibility that you are deceiving yourself. More importantly, honesty is the natural byproduct of a disciplined and energetic meditation practice. Meditation brings insight; therefore, honesty will develop naturally, without willful intention. This commitment to honesty — which may at first sound challenging and difficult — is in fact the only way to fully enjoy your life and to truly be yourself.

SINCERITY

Do everything sincerely. Sincerely feel what you are feeling. Sincerely see what you are seeing. Sincerely express who you are. Sincerely experience what you are interested in experiencing. Look at others sincerely. Sincerely have curiosity. It's okay. Whatever you do, just do it sincerely.

When a young child looks at you, there is always this quality of sincerity. No matter how closely she looks, you do not feel any judgment. You sense her curiosity. She is fully present, just looking. She sees all of your imperfections, but you are not embarrassed. You know she will not care about the size of your nose, the shape of your body, or the style of your dress. You are willing to be yourself because she sees you sincerely.

Sincerity is one of the most valuable things in life because it engenders innocence. When you view the world with innocence, everything is fresh. You appreciate and savor whatever you encounter. When you enjoy things innocently, you do not create negative consequences that will haunt you later.

How do you bring about this innocence? You cannot fake it. People will suspect your motives and will never trust you. Perfect innocence comes naturally only when you taste the richness of life. When you feel the preciousness of your every breath, you will not be distracted by promises of wealth or sensual pleasure. You will be enraptured by the wonder and beauty right under your nose. You will not be overpowered by any situation, and you will never feel intimidated.

In this very life, we hold a priceless jewel that should not be traded for anything. The sincere conviction that this life is truly worthwhile is what we need. This conviction, I feel, creates compassion and love for all beings. We cannot love falsely. When we love others and value their precious qualities, we will find real satisfaction and will not look for something in return.

To love others without expecting anything in return is sincere love. If you are expecting a reward, there is no innocence. If you act with a premeditated agenda, your love is insincere — it is not real. It is fabricated and contrived. Therefore, it is false.

It is not what you do that matters; it is how genuinely you do it. You will benefit from a spiritual path when you have sincerity. No matter what you do, you will find joy in it; this is the Buddha's promise. Your way of life will become very natural, very relaxed. Once everything is settled and you remain at ease, there will be nothing but light and clarity, nothing but bliss and freshness.

RESPECT

When we discover our true nature, we realize that we are fundamentally good and have nothing to hide from others. When we understand that there is no separate or abiding self that we need to protect or defend, we can navigate all the twists and turns of life with grace and poise. As we become less preoccupied with ourselves, our relationships become more healthy, open, and alive. Ultimately, a wholesome relationship with others is contingent on discovering our natural, innate wisdom. Wisdom is clear and naked awareness, which is innate and naturally present within all beings, even when it is obscured. When we uncover our buddha nature — our true essence — we feel profound regard and appreciation for all beings. Even when others have not actualized their true nature, we can see this potential, like a teacher recognizing the latent ability in a struggling student.

Everyone we meet becomes our teacher, our guide, and our inspiration. We always find some form of wisdom and decency in others, and we may be surprised to discover that everyone has something to offer. With every encounter, we can learn something new, and this enriches our lives. We can live in harmony with others while still accomplishing our goals.

Outwardly, people behave in helpful and harmful ways. Try not to fixate on their positive or negative actions; instead, look deeper and know that their basic nature is pure. Do not criticize or accuse, as this will make enemies out of friends. When we resent something our friend said yesterday, this is our mistake. We think our friend is the same person today as she was yesterday. With pure perception, we can see our friend with fresh and open eyes. When we focus on the past, we cast a shadow over the bright potential in each new moment.

Normally, we favor our friends and reject those who mistreat us. Focusing on our friends' good qualities, we favor them and view them in a biased way. We ignore strangers and feel hostility for our enemies. However, friends often become enemies, and enemies become friends. We should consider more deeply the motives for why people behave as they do and respond with patience and understanding.

Our dearest friends sometimes can be the most insincere. Friends can shower us with praise and admiration, and we become smug and complacent. We can learn from those who are forthright and direct. Hostile behavior from others gives us an opportunity to practice patience and strengthen our fortitude. It is wise not to be too fond of your friends or too disdainful of your enemies. The best approach is to view everyone equally, without bias, and to respect everyone always.

GENEROSITY

Giving with an open heart to those in need is an expression of generosity. However, if there is attachment to the one who gives, to the one who receives, or to the act of giving, this is not pure generosity. As long as one clings to the subtlest concept of giver or receiver, the act of giving is stained by dualistic attachment, like a beautiful work of calligraphy ruined by a little smudge of ink. True generosity is never tainted by this dualistic way of thinking, the mistaken perception of a substantially existing "I" and a substantially existing "other." If you give in this ordinary way, you may benefit the recipient, but you will not experience the unadulterated joy that comes from an act of giving that is free from "me" and "you." True generosity can lead one to the threshold of awakening because it is based on the reality that there is nothing to hold on to, no truly existing giver or receiver. The act of giving is completely authentic, and the "one" who gives does not expect thanks or reward.

You can be generous when you recognize the legitimacy of each thought as it arises. When you are present in the moment, you will experience the essence of each thought clearly. Do not ignore a single thought. If you are alert and aware of each thought, there will be no chance for dualistic thinking to take root. You may believe that your concept of "I" is more valid than anything else, but "I" is no more legitimate than "other." "Mine" is no more legitimate than "yours." Dualistic thinking simply creates the illusion of division, an illusion that disappears when you are truly present in the moment.

With this keen level of awareness, you can fly like the mythical *garuda*, which can soar through the sky as soon as it hatches from the egg. The *garuda* symbolizes true freedom and the unobstructed nature of enlightened wisdom. To be generous is to be totally free, not bound by any thought or perception. In this open state of mind, suppose you are enjoying a cup of tea. "You" are not having tea. The taste is not "yours." The tea is not "tea"! These are just labels. When the perceiver and perceived are not separate, there is nothing but bliss. Suppose you are having a passionate relationship, but you are not constrained by hopes or expectations. Nothing is holding you back; you are totally immersed in the moment. Imagine the freedom and delight you will feel! This is the expression of true generosity.

Caring for oneself is also an expression of generosity. If you understand how precious your life is, you will allow yourself the time and space in which to relax and appreciate your world. Like a refreshing breeze on a summer evening, you will feel the comfort of resting in your breath. You are a true friend to yourself when you can liberate the causes of stress. When you make mistakes, you can forgive yourself. If you spill coffee on your shirt, you do not have to be embarrassed. Mistakes will happen. Failure will happen. Failure is not condemned as something bad. Ultimately, no one ever fails, because our true nature is inherently good.

SIMPLICITY

It is not possible to live fully by indulging ourselves, chasing every whim and satisfying every desire. True practitioners of this path see the futility of overindulgence and the senselessness of endless distraction. They are content with very little because they understand the true value of their lives. They know that the more they have, the more they will want. The great masters of this tradition were intelligent people who could have achieved great material wealth if they so wished, but instead they chose to live simply and follow a path truly worthy of their time and attention.

In our tradition, the great masters shunned the world of personal gain and social status and lived in a carefree way. They were spurred on by the conviction that there is nothing of enduring value in the mundane world. In secluded settings, they had the freedom to explore their minds and test their mettle. They did not get entangled in their thoughts and emotions. They did not skate on the thin ice of ego, so they never fell into icy waters. This is how they mastered their minds and their energy.

We tend to become slaves of our thoughts and emotions. This is "my" loved one. This is "my" desire. This is "my" hope. This is "my" joy. We are in a prison of our own making. We rely too heavily on the external world for happiness and fulfillment. This dependence only makes us weaker. To gain strength, we must be willing to confront ourselves by looking within.

It may not be practical for everyone to emulate the great masters and live in an isolated cave on the mountainside. However, we can endeavor to live freely and simply from day to day. Determine what you truly need. You may discover that you can be comfortable and content with much less than you imagined. Cleanse yourself of attachment to material possessions, and resist becoming consumed with trivial matters.

One day at a time, see if you can live without being controlled by anger, attachment, jealousy, or pride. If you can remain content with yourself, you can achieve peace and comfort very easily. Give yourself time to breathe and appreciate your life. When you are living simply and have more space, ask yourself these profound questions: *Why am I here? What is my purpose? What is meaningful?*

If you can be content with yourself and handle your mind, this is all you need. We face an endless stream of thoughts and emotions, but we can relate to them skillfully, with continual awareness. This alone will keep us engaged.

We chase after unrequited love or jockey for a promotion at work. We surround ourselves with friends and loved ones in hopes of finding comfort and security. Most of our lives are spent looking for peace and happiness outside of our own minds and hearts. This is the source of our problems and the cause of our discontentment. If you can effectively master your mind and manage your life, this is more than enough. You are successful.

OPENNESS

The essence of compassion is open, vast, and all-embracing. Compassion is not just a matter of feeling empathy and doing good deeds. Of course, we should always aspire to help others, but there are greater and more profound ways to manifest compassion. Until the attainment of enlightenment, we will be limited in our capacity to benefit others, despite whatever progress we have made on our spiritual journey. Before awakening, everything we do is limited in some way, including the expression of compassion.

Generating compassion for others progressively sharpens our intelligence, opens our minds, and widens our vista. One should be receptive to new ideas and experiences. If we are interested in finding enduring happiness and in benefiting others, we have to broaden our vision. We should examine and question our preconceptions and be daring enough to explore new and unfamiliar terrain. We should not be so selective. A cherry-picking approach will limit our outlook, thwarting opportunities for authentic inquiry and profound realization.

It is our responsibility to be open and responsive to every situation. If we sense that we are closing down, we can relax and come back to our breath. We should reflect and determine why we are hesitating and holding back — why we are poised to dive into life, but then balk at the last moment. We should be eager to learn from every interaction and every challenge because everything in our lives has meaning. Nothing is inconsequential. Every moment is unique and meaningful. Let us cherish each moment and live as fully as we can.

Confidence

At the beginning of the path, Buddhism teaches us about the supreme value of human life. During the course of our journey, we are encouraged to make use of this precious opportunity with joyful effort. At the culmination, we find fulfillment in awakened activity for the benefit of others. The Buddha's true achievement is the realization of the preciousness of human life. His teachings show us how to draw the utmost value from our lives — how to recognize and actualize this priceless gift.

When you have conviction in the preciousness of life, you will have complete confidence in the moment. The context of each new situation will be clear, so there will be nothing that you cannot navigate skillfully. You will find fulfillment and resolution in every breath, so there will be nothing further to achieve. If you cannot unwind in the quiet movements of your breath, you are lost. Lacking a sense of completeness, you feel needy and insecure. There is so much you want to acquire and so much you need to accomplish. You crave a bigger house, more fashionable clothes, and a faster car. You feel awkward and self-conscious because you have drifted away from your natural way of being. You enter a perpetual cycle of self-justification from which you cannot escape.

When you are truly integrated with the flow of your breath, you will know that all beings are blessed with this same precious gift. You will trust in your goodness and in the basic decency of others. This conviction and confidence will prompt those around you to slow down and relax and to experience their lives in a complete way.

CHAPTER FOUR

This Precious Moment

Being Present in the Breath

Can we fully appreciate the intrinsic value of our human life and the preciousness of being alive? What makes us dissatisfied and convinces us that we need to chase after so many worldly goals and collect so many possessions? If we cannot relax in our breath and appreciate our being, we will feel compelled to look elsewhere and reach for something more.

We may have a family, our work, and other legitimate concerns. These things are important, but we need to remind ourselves that our activities should help to liberate us, not enslave us. When we recognize the preciousness of being, nothing will bind or burden us. Nothing will mean more to us than the freedom to breathe. Nothing will make us happier than being present in the breath, *fully in this moment*. We call this wakefulness.

Knowing hundreds of scriptures by heart is not wakefulness. Wakefulness is living unconditionally and utilizing every moment of your life in a meaningful way. It is legitimizing your every breath. When you have this understanding, you are heir to the Buddha's realization.

In-the-moment wakefulness is the key. Relaxing in the breath means just this: pausing continually through the course of your day to relish the miracle of breath, to appreciate its liveliness, to celebrate the moment without adding or subtracting anything. Being fully in the moment need be no more complicated than this.

Divorced from this wakeful awareness, our unruly emotions can easily consume us. We engage in unwholesome actions as we struggle to protect and enhance our sense of a separate self. We turn away from our essence and feel weak and unworthy. We forget that we have this wakeful nature, a wish-fulfilling jewel.[1] If we can live fully, enjoying the richness and beauty of life, we will have no regrets, even at the moment of death. Each breath, even our final breath, will be complete.

---

1. In Indian mythology, a wish-fulfilling jewel grants anything one could wish for. The wish-fulfilling jewel represents one's awakened nature and the capacity to fully benefit oneself and others.

Precious Human Birth

You cannot put a price tag on human life, our most precious endowment. As humans, we can think and feel more deeply than other beings. We yearn to lead a fulfilling life, and we feel incomplete and empty if we cannot succeed.

Over the course of a day, how many times are we conscious of the fact that we are breathing? In hospitals around the world, countless people are on the brink of death and struggling to breathe. Millions of people around the world have nothing to eat and are dying of starvation. Countless others are helpless victims of earthquakes, typhoons, and floods. Wars and civil strife plague the world, leaving tens of thousands suffering. How often do we think, "I am thankful that I am breathing today?" If we contemplate in this way, we will feel very rich, regardless of the size of our pocketbook, the trophies in our display case, or the jewels in our safe-deposit box. Remember, there will come a day, not too far away, when we will breathe our last breath, like a river running dry. So, let us breathe fully now.

How often are we aware of our natural endowments, the miraculous gifts that we normally take for granted? Most of us are lucky in that we can see, we can hear, we can feel, and we can reason. How fortunate we are! Most of us are born with two hands and ten fingers. It sounds very simple, but unless we reflect in this way, we will not appreciate these hands that can cook, write, touch, and reach out to others — we might even forget that we have these amazing hands!

There are a staggering seven billion humans inhabiting this earth. How many have lost their hearing or eyesight? How many will never see a sunset or hear the song of a nightingale? How many are mentally impaired and cannot benefit from spiritual teachings? How many are disillusioned and cynical after achieving material success? How many live in palatial homes, wandering from room to room, year in and year out, finding no satisfaction there? Reflect on the overwhelming number of people who have never heard the words of the enlightened masters and who have no reliable spiritual guide.

In these ways, and in any other way you can imagine, contemplate the preciousness of life. Remember, with every passing moment, you are expending your breath — your most valuable asset. When you are unaware of the preciousness of breath, there is little possibility of fulfilling your true potential. We cannot live our lives fully when we take this miracle of life for granted. Not appreciating the life that pulsates through our bodies is a sign that our minds are lost in distraction and drifting far away from the present moment. This triggers confusion and dissatisfaction. True contentment can be experienced only if we are *here with ourselves fully*.

Think of the many different ways in which this life has inherent value and richness. We have to meditate on the freedoms and advantages of this human life. You will become brighter and more alert. As you gain more insight, you will experience fewer obstacles, less turmoil, and greater ease. When you truly appreciate your own life, you will inspire others with your passion and zest for living. Every moment, you will be astonished to be alive!

Blind to our inner wealth, we are easily tempted and seduced by fleeting attractions. Popular culture and television advertisements bombard us with products that will allegedly make us happier — shampoo for silkier hair, cars with more horsepower, clothes for an attractive look — but all of these things provide us with only a veneer of comfort and pleasure.

What is the purpose of life? How can we discover meaning in seeming chaos, and how do we find fulfillment? Will accumulating wealth and globetrotting make us happy? How many beaches can we relax on? After all, beaches are all the same: sand, water, and sun! Let's be serious, no matter what we have — the most luxurious home, the most sumptuous food, or the most comfortable beachside chair — we soon grow bored. At some point, we will realize that the pleasure of material objects can never satisfy us completely. We will find true fulfillment in the unconditional state of our being. Recognizing our true nature will ensure complete and lasting satisfaction. We will not cling to passing pleasures; we will enjoy them as ornaments that embellish our inherently rich state of being. This is the true way.

Ultimately, those who are inseparable from their breath will enjoy fulfilling lives. You could wander across the seven continents, searching for excitement and pleasure, and end up feeling dispirited and exhausted. Sooner or later you have to return home and realize that you are simply a breathing human being. In the gentle flow of breath, everything settles into completeness, like the pieces of a puzzle put in their proper places.

If we think about it, we are not all that different. We are all breathing beings. We are all breathing the same air, whether we are wealthy entrepreneurs or destitute beggars. Regardless of race or status, we are equally the same breathing beings. To live fully, we need to cultivate great respect for everyone. Within the unconditional appreciation of our breath, we will find unconditional love for all beings. When we realize how precious our own breath is, we will not think of hurting anyone, not even a tiny ant running across our table.

We will not waste a single moment looking elsewhere. To be one with our true nature will be our only interest and our only desire. We will be gentle human beings who appreciate and respect the wonder of everyone's breath. This is the only worthy achievement in this fleeting life: to be a kind and caring being.

Cherish Life

If you live without mindfulness, you will experience many difficulties. Cycles of pain and dissatisfaction will keep on repeating over and over, like irritating songs on instant replay. You may ask yourself, "How can I find lasting joy and pleasure in this world?"

How can there be enduring happiness when all pleasures are conditional and temporary? Happiness that is dependent on causes and conditions is unstable; we can never expect it to last. For instance, we may enjoy delicious food and drink, but how long can we linger in this pleasure? Not for very long.

This is something worth contemplating. Do not measure yourself by how affluent, successful, or influential you are. Measure yourself by how content you are, by how present you can be in each moment.

Obsessively planning for tomorrow prevents you from appreciating the richness of this day. If you wish to fulfill your deepest aspirations, focus on being attentive to the moment. This is the best way to fulfill the purpose of your being. As you savor the present moment, you will truly breathe completely. The simple act of breathing in and out will suffuse you with a deep sense of satisfaction and gratitude. When you live fully in this profound way, you will discover that your breath is your single most precious gift and blessing.

PRICELESS BREATH

Visualize the last moment of your life, as you exhale your final breath. This will happen to all of us. While you vividly imagine your final moment, how could you allow yourself to breathe with anger or rage? How could you allow yourself to breathe with jealousy or pride? You could not breathe in such harmful ways! When others cause us harm, they deserve our compassion, since they, too, are spending their priceless breath every second. No matter how harmfully they appear to behave, they do not deserve our vengeance, and we should not waste our precious breath dwelling in negativity.

Regardless of the wealth and possessions we accumulate, at the time of death we cannot take a single penny with us. At that moment, search the world over to see if you can buy just ten more breaths of life. We cannot plead with our friend, "I have a million dollars in my account — can you buy me ten more breaths?" The wealthiest man on earth cannot buy one more minute of life. Ask yourself, "What is my bank account worth to me now? How valuable is a moment of breath? How could I waste a single moment of this precious human life? How can I have the courage to live this life fully and meaningfully?"

One of my students recently spoke to me about his father's death. He spent several days by his father's bedside as his life slowly ebbed away. In stark contrast to his full and active life, his father was now unable to speak and painfully struggled with every breath. Heartbreaking as it was, the son felt that this was his father's final gift to him. His father was teaching him about the brevity and uncertainty of life and urging him to live in the most meaningful way.

We may believe we are living our lives fully when we frequent a popular French bistro for a delectable meal or an exclusive boutique for chic clothing. We may even study Buddhist teachings with a famous Tibetan lama[2] in an effort to live our lives fully. We are constantly attempting to find happiness. We all share this common experience; therefore, I have tremendous respect for everyone. We are journeying together, and this path is not an easy one. Until we discover the true nature of our being, we suffer. And we all suffer together.

When we glimpse our true nature, we recognize the preciousness of being. We keenly sense that the value of a single breath is beyond calculation. If we stop and examine it closely, we will recognize how valuable each and every breath is. We will find real satisfaction in this discovery and the passion to use our time well.

Breathing fully is living fully, and in the midst of a deep breath, life is full. So breathe joyfully and breathe completely. You will be content with everything just as it is, and see each moment as flawless and perfect. You will experience a childlike fascination with the world and have a love affair with every instant of your life.

---

2. *Lama* is a Tibetan honorific for one who has spiritual realization and is capable of guiding others. Lama ultimately means "mother of compassion."

CHAPTER FIVE

Whatever Arises Ceases

EMBRACING CHANGE

We generally have peculiar notions about death, especially in the West. Elegant funeral homes are comfortable and tastefully furnished. The corpse of the deceased is embalmed and then primped by the undertaker before it is presented in an open coffin. Cemeteries are scenic places with manicured lawns, colorful flowers, and meandering walkways. Perhaps our need to sanitize death is a reflection of our fear, our unwillingness to face mortality. We think of death as something dark and dreadful, something that has to be cleansed and made presentable, like tarnished silver in need of polish. Instead of accepting the reality of death and impermanence, we plan well into the future, as if we will live forever. However, the honest and courageous approach is to acknowledge the inevitability of death and embrace its imminence.

It can be unbearable to face the fact that, sooner or later, we will die and lose every single thing that we cherish. We may manage to control the external conditions of our environment for most of our lives, but we have no control over the time and place of death, just as we have no control over the passing of days and nights.

We cannot expect the young to live beyond the aged. There are grandparents who grieve for the death of a grandchild. Young and old can die suddenly — struck by disease or a fatal accident. Some experience gradual decline with physical or mental disorders. Others enjoy good health, but, as the years pass, they slowly lose their vitality and inch closer to death, like the leaves of a tree turning brittle and brown as winter approaches. Our vibrant energy gradually disappears. Bedridden, we are powerless to move and reduced to skin and bones. In the prime of our lives we may have been great athletes or dancers, but at this point we are helpless.

The impermanence of life is powerful and inescapable. Although we make plans for our lives well into the future, nothing is certain. This life is precious, but there is no assurance that we will live for one more day.

Try to embrace death without flinching. Acknowledge the certainty of death without fear. Heightened awareness of impermanence stirs up the passion to live fully. In Buddhism, much emphasis is placed on impermanence and death, but the intent is not to create fear, dread, or panic. On the contrary, awareness of death leads us to appreciate each moment of our lives completely.

A line from a Buddhist prayer reads:

Inexorably, death closes in, never pausing for even an instant.

Do you know for certain when, where, or how you will die? Can you be sure that you will not die right now? Between one breath and the next, there is no guarantee that death will not slip in. To awaken in the morning still breathing and healthy is truly miraculous! Yet we take this miracle completely for granted.

When you are aware of impermanence, you will be more fearless and more caring. You will not withhold your feelings. When you are alert to the real possibility that tomorrow may never come, you will express your love for others now. You will feel grateful for every moment and abide in the purity of the present.

Deep in our hearts, we all know that death is tenaciously

waiting. But we close our eyes, and we rarely allow our outlook on life to be touched in a positive way by the reality of impermanence. Isn't it interesting how we so easily forget that those who harm us will one day face death too? Given the brevity and impermanence of life, have we ever thought of letting our opponent win the argument, keep the trophy, or claim the victory? When we concede victory, we will not lose. Rather, we can celebrate the freedom that comes with awareness of the transient nature of all things.

THE SUPREME MEDITATION

In order to make the best use of your time, contemplate the truth of impermanence. Be ever mindful that your life is perishable. Never forget the indisputable truth of the transience of all phenomena. You will not progress in your practice without this foundation, just as you will not progress in algebra without first understanding arithmetic.

The Buddha taught his disciples that reflection on impermanence is the supreme meditation. Every subtle change in our thoughts and perceptions is a lesson on the momentary nature of appearances. If the truth of change is not foremost in our minds, we are likely to be ruled by disturbing emotions and negativity will consume us.

There are innumerable metaphors that illustrate the fleeting nature of life. Life is like a rainbow, so beautiful and colorful one moment, and in the next moment nonexistent! Dewdrops sparkle in the evening moonlight, but swiftly evaporate in the warmth of the morning sun. Life is like a candle in the wind; at any moment the flame could be extinguished, leaving us in darkness. That is how uncertain and short our lives are!

There are countless ways to reflect on impermanence. We all have personal experiences that plainly demonstrate our vulnerability. Your parents may have passed away after living an active life; your brother may have died in a sudden accident; or your cat may have expired in her sleep. Displays of death and impermanence are everywhere.

When my grandmother was very old, she gradually became debilitated as her body swelled with water. There was nothing the local doctors could do for her, and no drugs were available to relieve her excruciating pain. My grandmother was a wise, spirited, and competent woman who was always prepared to confront every challenge. But at that time, our quiet dwelling was filled with her cries of agony, day and night. As my grandmother had instructed me before her illness, I read aloud from the *Tibetan Book of the Dead*, a guide for those facing death. To watch my beloved grandmother suffer in this way made a strong impression on me. It was a vivid example of how painful dying can be and how powerless we are in the face of death.

Consider the possibility that your life could end in a sudden accident. Think for a moment, "There was a plane crash and everyone died. I could have been on that flight. My life could be over!" Billions of beings have lived on this earth — where are they now? Most have long been forgotten, as will we be forgotten with the passing of time. When death summons us, in an instant everything will vanish, and no one will remember how rich, powerful, or influential we were. These reflections should not cause despair. Rather, they should revitalize our strength and revive our zest for living.

Reflecting on the certainty of death jolts us from our stupor. It helps awaken us to the preciousness of life, ensuring that we *never take it for granted*. We should make the most of the opportunities that life provides us each and every day. At the time of death, we will be overwhelmed with fear and burdened with regret if we do not take care of ourselves now. If we do not live this life meaningfully, we are losing a precious opportunity to become genuine and dignified beings. If we can live with awareness and use our time well, we will depart this life gracefully and courageously, without looking back.

Just a Short Stay

This life of ours is like a brief stay at a hotel. We paid for a nice little room, which is our good fortune. Perhaps we could even afford a suite at a five-star hotel. Either way, we have comfortable shelter, and in this sense we are lucky. Very soon we will be checking out.

During our short stay, wouldn't it be wise to relax and enjoy a peaceful rest? However, as soon as we settle down, we begin to see faults in our hotel room. There is a crack in a wall, so we go to the hardware store to buy some plaster. Some time later, after the wall is patched up, we notice that the color does not match, so we return to the store for paint and spend a few hours painting the wall. Then we find that the room's décor is not to our liking, so we move the rug and rearrange the furniture. Tired from all our exertion, we lie down for a nap, but the mattress is lumpy, so we run down to the store to buy a new mattress. On returning, we discover that the toilet in the bathroom is leaking. By the time we fix the plumbing, the sun is setting and our stay is over.

Now it is time to check out. Unfortunately, we were not able to relax, and we leave the hotel feeling tired and grumpy. This is how we misuse our lives, forgetting that our time here is brief and fleeting, and that nothing is more valuable than having a restful stay. How much should we rely on our worldly affairs and material possessions? How much should we invest in conditions that are unstable and constantly changing?

You must reach a turning point where you become very practical. During your brief sojourn, try not to make too much fuss about flaws in your hotel room, in your life. Whatever presents itself in this very moment is *it*. If your car breaks down in the middle of the road, you can respond appropriately and not waste your time lamenting. If your boss is having a temper tantrum and is swearing at you, it is quite all right, for after all, bosses do get angry. If there is nothing you can do to change your boss's angry temperament, why get upset? Without awareness, one will never be able to handle relative circumstances gracefully. Let's not waste our breath trying to change what already is. Do not invest too much time in what can never bring lasting fulfillment.

CHAPTER SIX

Identity Crisis

Territorial Self

For thousands of years, human beings have grappled with an existential crisis:

They have killed millions of people to prove that they exist.

They have built millions of structures to prove that they exist.

They have created hundreds of religions to prove that they exist.

They have manufactured guns and knives to prove that they exist.

They have gorged on food and drink to prove that they exist.

They have laughed and cried and danced to prove that they exist.

But it is still unclear whether anyone knows if he or she truly exists.

To confirm our sense of self, we philosophize and theorize, construct and destroy, consume and indulge, but in the end, the nature of our existence remains unclear. This uncertainty compels us to squander our time in futile and wearisome activities. We feel insecure and we want to believe that our cherished "self" is tangible and permanent. We desperately long to define ourselves, and so we create arbitrary identities that only limit our potential and leave us feeling bewildered.

We create standards for ourselves and for others. We cling to what we like, feel aversion for what we dislike, and ignore everything else. We establish boundaries, and our habitual thoughts reinforce our sense of a territorial self. Emotional obstacles do not spring from out of the blue; they are fueled by our belief in an autonomous self that is separate from everything else. We build more and more fences, and we create more and more yardsticks with which to measure the world. We have more and more terrain to protect and defend. Trapped behind walls of our own making, we find it difficult to be caring and kind, and we are reluctant to trust others.

When we are self-absorbed in our own territory, even the simple act of drinking coffee can become poisonous. Many of us feel that we cannot function without our first cup of coffee in the morning. Without our usual morning java, we grow upset and irritable. When our habitual thoughts and actions define and limit us, we are not able to live in the moment.

You can begin to dismantle the stronghold of the territorial self when you care more for others. Skillfully relate to your thoughts and examine your motivation at all times, even when doing something as simple as sipping a cup of coffee. Try drinking without any selfish motive, while mindful of the needs of others. Then your coffee will be like nectar, a taste of your basic goodness, which is beyond the limited self and is not bound by habit. To skillfully elevate your thinking is the key!

Shattering Attachment

All experience is like an illusion, like a dream. Within this expansive dream, many small dreams are appearing and dissolving simultaneously. Recognizing the nature of experience as dreamlike is our best protection against pain and distress.

If you are growing attached to your beautiful friend or getting angry with your demanding boss, remind yourself that the nature of experience is dreamlike. Although appearances seem to be substantial, whatever occurs in your life does not last beyond this moment.

We hypnotize ourselves with the comforting impression of permanence and stability and are deceived by our own trickery. We grow dependent on our friends and our loved ones. The intelligent thing to do is to dismantle our false beliefs and misperceptions. It is wise to shatter our attachments by reflecting on the ephemeral and capricious nature of our thoughts and emotions. Amid all of this instability and uncertainty, draw strength by remembering that our true essence is immutable and unaffected by change. It is unconditional; therefore, it cannot be destroyed. However, all relative appearances are subject to causes and conditions and are invariably impermanent.

If you are a willing participant in your own deception, sooner or later, reality will wake you up. When your illusions collapse like a house of cards, it could break your heart. Since you are not prepared to tackle all of life's sudden and inevitable changes, you could find it unbearable. From the outset, if you are awake and watchful, you can shatter your illusions on the spot. Perhaps your heart won't be broken, even when everything falls apart.

Free from the Notion of Self

Being genuine, which means being true to who we are, is possible only when we are free from the illusion of an independently existent self. Ordinarily, as human beings, we do not actualize our highest potential, our buddha nature. Instead, we embrace our confusion. When we recognize that this limited and confused self has no foundation at all, we can embrace what is clear and empty as our true self. Embracing our true nature, nothing can obscure or limit us in any given moment. This is who we are: *limitless and complete in our existence.*

We think we are free, but we are bound by our fears and delusions — by all of our self-made constraints. We do not have trust and confidence in our true nature, and therefore we are incomplete.

If the nature of the self is empty, does that mean that nothing exists? Have you ever looked at a lotus flower in full bloom? You might be intoxicated with its radiant beauty. At the height of its freshness, you cannot find a single speck of impurity, imperfection, or decay. It is flawless and pristine. This is what emptiness is: *empty of all defilement and obscuration.* Be clear about this: emptiness is not a state of blankness, darkness, or nothingness. The natural state of emptiness is replete with good qualities. It is free of all distortion, so one can see everything exactly as it is.

When the mind is empty of obscuration, it is lucidly clear and open. With a clear mind, all of your expressions will be genuine and your communication will be natural — free from hesitation or holding back. Your bearing will always have the mark of authenticity. If you try to wear a mask, your diamond-like awareness will shatter it, right on the spot. The diamond is a symbol of indestructible clarity, which eradicates all deception. The mind can perceive clearly when not obscured by discursive thinking and disturbing emotions. This clarity is an intrinsic and natural quality of the mind. It is not created by conditions; therefore, it can never be destroyed.

Examine your mind and attempt to discover the nature of this so-called self. Can you find an owner of your experiences, a thinker of your thoughts who is truly there? Does such a self exist? Or do you merely find intangible thoughts, feelings, and perceptions that are fleeting and impermanent?

While everything appears in the mind, neither the mind nor what appears in the mind comprise objective or substantial reality. All of our thoughts and perceptions are ephemeral. If we believe that our projections are real, we will view everything in our world as truly existing, just as it appears. Whatever occurs in our lives is like a dream. All experience is intangible and beyond our grasp. For the most part, we mistakenly view this dream as real, but the appearances of this life are like the conjuring of a master magician. We are fooled by appearances that are dream-like and fleeting. Indeed, it is time to wake up!

Consider a young child looking at the reflection of the moon in a lake. The child will think that the moon exists in the water, and it is difficult to convince the child otherwise. When the child grows older and wiser, you can point your finger and explain, "That is the actual moon, and this is a reflection in the water." However, from the Buddhist perspective, the appearance of the moon in the sky is insubstantial, and so is the person pointing at the moon. This is not so easy for us to accept, but it is essential to understand. It is our misconception to believe that our perceptions, thoughts, and emotions have substantial existence. This confused view of things becomes our enemy. For instance, feelings of anger and hatred can become entrenched in our minds, lasting for days, months, or years.

Inwardly we feel impoverished, so we crave many things. Engaging in business, we work hard to make a profit, and in the short term, we may feel that we have succeeded. But we do not realize that the profit we make is like an illusion. In other words, when we solidify our notion of self, we solidify our notion of profit. We think the "I" exists; therefore "I" must make a profit. This "I" is ego. Working hard to satisfy the ego, we corrupt our natural energy with selfish thinking. It is better to let the energy release and flow naturally. If we think we have gained something, what does it matter? If we think we have lost something, what does it matter? We create notions of gain and loss, but in truth, they have no substantial basis. It is all dreamlike and illusory.

When we awake from a pleasant dream, we might cling to our dream experience, but we know it is not real. If we develop insight into the nature of self and appearances, we will clearly recognize that this life is like a dream. Whatever we envision is like a mirage, and in the end, we cannot hold on to anything. This moment is like an appearance of the shining moon in the water; it is vivid, but it is merely a reflection. We cannot hold on to this moment, but we can value and experience this moment fully, while knowing there is nothing to cling to.

DISCOVERING THE TRUE SELF

L oving oneself could be considered selfish, if there is a so-called self that is solid and unchanging, never willing to budge. However, the best way to love oneself is to realize one's essence, which is the true self.

What is the true self? Your true self is revealed in every moment. You cannot isolate and identify a self that exists apart from your experience. Your true self is not separate from your experience, just as waves are not separate from the ocean. When you have a good thought, this energy is the expression of true self. When you have a bad thought, this energy is also the expression of true self. When you love someone, this is the display of true self. When you hate someone, this is also the display of true self. When you understand the nature of true self, you will experience an unobstructed flow of energy, and the essence of this energy is who you are. There is no single, autonomous, independent "I." When we believe in a truly existing "I," we become selfish and try to hold on to this presumed "self." We do not want to die because we have built ourselves up and convinced ourselves that we have so much to lose. It is like children building sand castles on the beach and becoming so enchanted by their creations that they cry when the waves sweep them away. Nearby, their grand-father smiles, as he understands the shifting tides and the fragile nature of sand castles.

To love yourself is to nurture your understanding and realize your true self. In modern psychology, the notion of loving one-self can be somewhat questionable. According to many psychologists, you can deconstruct a negative image you have of yourself and replace it with a more positive one. A psychologist may say, "Love yourself and tell me everything." If the patient feels inadequate, the psychologist attempts to help the patient build a more satisfying self-image. But this can be likened to dismantling one sand castle and building a grander, more beautiful castle. Soon the waves will wash this edifice away, since everything is impermanent. Whatever is born is bound to die, including our conditional notions of self. However, if you recognize with total awareness that all experience is the flow of natural, unobstructed energy — the expression of your true self — you will be free to tango with this energy. You can dance quite skillfully without a selfish agenda. Actualizing this state is the most important thing. There is nothing better than that because you will be physically, mentally, and emotionally fit. And, more importantly, you will also be spiritually fit.

CHAPTER SEVEN

Facing Obstacles and Obscurations

BEYOND FIXATION

From one point of view, the practice of the spiritual path can be very simple. The essence of the mind is beyond all complexity, but it is easy for the mind to get lost and wander in a bewildering maze of thoughts and feelings. Therefore, we encounter obstacles and obscurations on our spiritual path. These apparent hurdles are not to be shunned. Rather, they become the working basis for spiritual growth.

Why do we encounter conflict when interacting with others? The answer lies in our tendency to be selfish. In the office we might ingratiate ourselves with our supervisor in the hopes of gaining a promotion. Or we might be dishonest with our friend, afraid of losing her favor. Self-absorption prohibits open and honest communication. When wrapped up tight in our own narrow interests, we try to manipulate and control everything. If we want to relate skillfully with others, we should not be self-centered. Then we can communicate in an honorable and straightforward way.

When we comprehend that the notions of "self" and "other" do not truly exist as separate and distinct entities, there will be no grounds for conflict. We can communicate directly, without currying favor or fearing harm to our ego. We can express indignation without being defensive or aggressive. We all experience anger, jealousy, and pride, but they are not the main culprits. The source of conflict is an exaggerated belief in this so-called self.

When we cling to this perception of "self," we create the perception of "other." When there is "self" and "other," there is "mine" and "yours," my family and your family, my home and your home, my country and your country. This is dualistic fixation, the root of all conflict and misery in the world. Those who are genuinely interested in creating a more peaceful world will seek to tame their egos and conquer the destructive forces of dualistic fixation.[1]

We should aspire to abide in the purity of the nondual state, free from the confusion of "self" and "other." This is our natural abode, beyond all dualistic fixations. One releases the tensions of body and mind brought on by the conflict of dualistic extremes. Then the reference points of "this" and "that" will not impede the natural flow of energy. If you take your friend out to dinner, you are more likely to enjoy your time together without any expectations. If you have a wonderful time, that is fine. If nothing special happens, that is fine, too.

A stockbroker on Wall Street could lose his composure, anxiously watching the rapid fluctuations on the ticker, or he could transcend the dualism of "up" and "down" by flowing with the numbers. He could view the swings of the market and his rapid calculations as an exhilarating dance, refusing to let the fluctuations of hope and fear sap his energy and undermine his confidence. The numbers will always go up and down. He could spend his entire life trying to stay one step ahead of the market, but in the end he will have squandered his precious time and resources in exchange for mere financial gain.

---

1. Duality will be discussed in more detail in chapter 9.

Look to the Source

Destructive habits and careless behavior are the cause of our suffering. If we seek to live our lives fully, we should not become trapped in our routines. When a bee settles on a flower to suck its nectar, it is intoxicated by the taste. Unaware that night is descending, the bee is trapped in the flower as the petals slowly close. As human beings, we should use our intelligence and hone our awareness so that our habits do not shackle us and rob us of our freedom.

Discursive thoughts and afflictive emotions obscure the naturally expansive and luminous nature of mind. Awareness is lost when we narrowly focus on ourselves and what the "I" experiences. This tunnel vision creates the breeding ground for a strong sense of ego. When we cannot transcend our ordinary, habitual ways of thinking, we become mired in our confusion. Not recognizing the pristine nature of mind, we suffer, since there is a great deal of attachment to the "I." An endless stream of thoughts, with one thought linked to the next, traps us in a perpetual cycle of confusion and pain.

Each thought should remain in its own place. It would not make sense to drag a caterpillar from its cocoon and expect it to make honey; that would be unnatural. Similarly, if you placed a honeybee in a cocoon, it would not know how to transform into a butterfly. So, proverbially speaking, the caterpillar should remain in its cocoon, and the honeybee should make honey. When you experience each thought in its completeness, the energy of the thought arises and dissolves in its own place. Therefore, you do not need to tamper with your thoughts. Further elaboration causes bewilderment and confusion. When the energy of each thought is complete and independent, it is liberated upon arising and leaves no trace.

If you cannot see the nature of each thought as complete and independent, it is because you are attached to the "I" and what the "I" creates. When you think, "I am going to do this," you create continuity for this "I." If you think, "I want this," you mentally select one button, and if you think, "I want that," you select the next button. There is no space for each thought to be complete and independent because you are thriving on the illusion of continuity. One could say that an independent thought is natural energy that is fresh, vivid awareness. It is not dependent upon further support.

When you follow your thoughts in pursuit of an illusory "I," your entanglement with each thought enslaves you. This mental confusion compels you to follow the first thought with a second thought, the second thought with a third thought, and so on, and so on. Therefore, each thought does not exist independently. We write our own story based on an illusory self. Bound in an endless chain of confused thoughts, we suffer in a vicious cycle of misery, which we call samsara. Samsara is the state of unenlightened ignorance. Unaware of the pure nature of mind and experience, one is helplessly controlled by disturbing emotions and karma, and one experiences an endless stream of mental and physical stress and suffering.

During the practice of meditation, we experience gaps in the flow of thoughts, and this space allows us to relax and loosen the grip of entrenched habits and reactive behavior. Glimpses of space in our mental landscape slowly free us from a tangled web of discursive thoughts and allow us to live more fully in the luminous present. Meditation is an effective tool for breaking free of deep-seated habits. Other methods, such as those offered in some self-help books, attempt to replace negative habits with positive thinking, but this does not address the real source of the problem. If we wish to free ourselves from our habits, the most effective approach is to ask ourselves, "Who is bound by habit, and how do these habits originate?"

The frequently quoted metaphor of the lion and the dog illustrates this approach. If you throw a stone at a dog, the dog will chase after the stone. If you throw a stone at a lion, the lion will chase after you! The dog will continue to chase stones, but the lion will be finished with it once and for all. Look directly at the source of each thought rather than following its trail. Habits are conditional and fabricated by thoughts. These patterns of thought and action are the result of our failure to discover their source. Habits are a form of energy, and energy emerges and subsides like waves on the surface of the ocean. When you recognize the source, the energy will self-liberate upon arising; it will not result in more habitual behavior.

Your practice is to find the source of the stone. You can continue to behave like a restless dog chasing after each thought, or you can pounce like a fearless lion and discover that the source of your thoughts is pure energy arising from emptiness. In this state of timeless purity, nothing truly comes into existence and nothing solidly exists, so there is no obstruction. If you have the courage to rest in this vast space, the fictions that fuel your enslaving habits will find no fertile ground in which to grow.

We should not reject our thoughts and feelings, since they are all valid. However, our thoughts and feelings cause us problems when we cling to them as if they were fixed and unchanging. When we abide in the empty and spacious nature of self and phenomena, we are free from all confusion. Therefore, let everything arise as sheer inspiration. Let everything be a celebration. Whatever arises is perfectly fine, but if nothing arises, that is fine, too. With a flexible mind, we can direct our lives with sophistication. We will be beyond corruption, and no matter what happens, we will be above the fray, so to speak. When we recognize the luminous quality of our true nature, clear essence will appear everywhere. This is amazing indeed!

DISSOLVING EMOTIONAL AFFLICTIONS

In this tradition, we do not reject or accept anything outright. Without holding back, we must be willing to experience our feelings and emotions fully. They are all valid because they emerge from a wellspring of pure energy. However, when the machinations of ego corrupt this energy, like toxic smoke consuming a pure blue sky, emotions can quickly become poisonous. With pure awareness, the raw energy of the emotions will not cause harm. These disturbing emotions or afflictions are desire, anger, pride, envy, and ignorance.

DESIRE

We grasp for desirable sense objects. Obsessive desire, and the attachment that follows, is the fuel that ignites frustration, disappointment, and pain. The energy of desire in itself is neither good nor bad; however, when it is poisoned with possessiveness, it becomes the cause of suffering. The need to possess grows out of a fissure in our perception: the desiring subject feels separate from the desired object, causing feelings of impoverishment and neediness. When attracted to seemingly external objects, our minds can easily become inflamed with desire.

The antidote for obsessive desire and attachment is generosity. One could say that generosity is freedom from attachment and having the capacity to give openly without expecting something in return. The Buddha taught that the one who practices perfect generosity never feels the need to possess or be attached to any object. On the highest level, the supreme form of generosity is to embrace all beings as they are, without the slightest trace of self-centered bias or judgment. Impartial concern and genuine caring for others are peerless generosity.

Begin by being more generous with your possessions, your time, and your heart. For many of us, giving generously without holding back does not come naturally. Here is a practice that a wise master gave to a miserly man who found it difficult to be generous.

First, think about what you are most attached to, such as your favorite food or an expensive watch. Visualize that object in your right hand. In your left hand, visualize someone in need of this object. Without hesitation, pass the object from your right hand to the person in your left hand, and imagine him or her enjoying and benefiting from your generous gift. Partake in their joy and happiness. Repeat this practice again and again, and you will cultivate a generous heart.

This is a simple but effective practice that can help you grow accustomed to giving freely. You will begin to appreciate the joy that comes from giving. The practice of generosity is a powerful way to counteract the mind of attachment.

The power of the sun can create electricity for our good use, but it can also burn our skin. When we harness the sun's energy intelligently, we benefit from light, even on the darkest of nights. While the pure energy of the sun is neither good nor bad, the way we use its power determines whether the results will be helpful or harmful.

The energy of desire can steer us in a helpful or harmful direction. If we cannot direct this energy with the positive intentions of a generous heart, we will follow our selfish ways. With a noble spirit, we can channel our desire into our practice, aspiring to attain enlightenment for the benefit of others.

If we can recognize the desired object as none other than the display of radiant awareness, we can liberate desire. Each of the five disturbing emotions can be purified and transformed into their five corresponding wisdoms. According to the Vajrayana[2] Buddhist teachings, desire is transformed into *discriminative wisdom*, and manifests as empathy and compassion for others. With discriminative wisdom, we recognize that the energy of desire and the object of our desire are not separate or distinct. In this way, our understanding transforms the poison of desire into the nectar of wisdom.

ANGER

We feel frustrated when we cannot obtain what we want or when we encounter what we dislike. Frustration can easily lead to anger, like a small spark setting off a raging forest fire. Those who prevent us from attaining what we desire are likely to provoke our anger, and someone who attacks our cherished beliefs can spark resentment, irritation, or rage.

Patience is the antidote for anger. The word for "patience" in Tibetan means "able to bear." When we cannot pause in the space between the object of our irritation and our angry response, we are not able to bear a situation with patience. Resting in this space is imperative. Otherwise, we react impulsively and

---

2. The three Buddhist paths are Hinayana, Mahayana, and Vajrayana. The Vajrayana path utilizes powerful methods to swiftly lead, within this lifetime, to full enlightenment.

cannot view the object of our irritation with equanimity. When we fail to practice patience, we attack or defend in a stream of angry outbursts.

As with desire, the energy that fuels our anger is pure. In our practice, we do not suppress or unleash the energy of anger, but recognize its uncorrupted source. The corruption comes from ego, with its likes and dislikes, with its hopes and fears. In recognizing the untainted, unconditional nature of this energy, anger is pacified and transformed into *mirror-like wisdom*. Just as a mirror reflects images precisely, mirror-like wisdom sees the nature of all things without distortion. Anger is transformed into clarity.

PRIDE

Feeling insignificant and insecure, we typically compensate by projecting a façade of superiority. A boy who resents his brother's accomplishments loses sight of his own potential; he may lash out at his brother by boasting that he is smarter and stronger. Pride grows when we lack the *wisdom of equality*, which perceives the sameness of all phenomena. Free from the limitations of ego, we discover inherent strength and richness. We are confident in mind's innate capacity and power. This power dwells equally within all beings, so there is no need to create or be bound to hierarchies of any kind.

Like the Buddha himself, those who are the most content exhibit the least pride. The Buddha was a prince who relinquished all his worldly wealth and influence without hesitation, in pursuit of spiritual attainment. He gave what he had to the poor, retained only a loincloth, and withdrew to the forest to meditate. He understood the true potential of the mind and harnessed its power in a perfect way.

When we harness this power within us, we will never feel

weak or inadequate. We will not be inclined to do useless or silly things, like surrendering to the empty trappings of wealth or fame. Outward appearances will not manipulate or seduce us in any way because we enjoy inherent wealth and splendor. With this level of confidence, we experience vajra-pride.[3]

Vajra-pride is not ordinary pride; it is an endless source of inspiration and richness. Beyond self-conceit and arrogance is the vajra-pride of realization, with full confidence in your indestructible quality. You have the strength to conquer every obstacle. You are free from any trace of false pride and will never feel superior to others.

ENVY

Envy is a hindrance to both material and spiritual success. What is the nature of envy, and how does it originate? Like the other afflictive emotions, the essence of envy is fundamentally pure, and it is known as *all-accomplishing wisdom*, or the capacity to effortlessly accomplish every goal. When we cherish ourselves above everyone else, our own selfish desires always come first. We grow envious of those who appear to enjoy more happiness, success, or adulation. We resent our neighbors' good fortune, feeling like their accomplishments belittle our own.

Modifying our attitude can help us to purify the destructive energy of envy. We can make it our practice to always wish the best for others and take pleasure in their happiness and good fortune. If we are mindful, we can spot envy as it arises and redirect our energy in a positive way. Unimpeded by the

---

3. *Vajra* is a Sanskrit word meaning diamond-like or indestructible. Vajra-pride is confidence in one's pure, unchanging nature, which is not corrupted by the arrogance of ego.

affliction of envy, spontaneous energy fulfills the wishes and satisfies the needs of both self and others.

IGNORANCE

We have discussed four of the five afflictions: desire, anger, pride, and envy. All are born from the affliction of ignorance. Ignorance is the root of all the disturbing emotions, and in this context, it is a lack of integration with the pure energy that is the basis of all experience. With the dawning of wisdom, energy is not distorted by the ego. When the obscuring forces of ignorance are purified, the *wisdom of all-pervading space* is revealed. The disturbing emotions in their purified form are the five wisdoms, a sacred realm of joy and freedom. Listed together, these are:

Discriminative wisdom
Mirror-like wisdom
The wisdom of equality
All-accomplishing wisdom
The wisdom of all-pervading space

CONQUERING YOUR ENEMIES

Breathe deeply, without dwelling on thoughts of the past, present, or future. What else do we need, beyond this capacity to breathe deeply? Your breath is your true friend because breath is inseparable from you. Everything else will leave you, fall apart, and disappear. Only your breath will remain inseparable.

Within each breath, there is the essence of the warrior. Spiritual warriors do not brandish machine guns and hand grenades, intent on conquering external enemies. They are not interested in destroying anything. Rather, they are determined to understand what is destroying them. Anger, desire, pride, envy, and ignorance are the warrior's real enemies. Spiritual warriors go to battle with their afflictive emotions. They are committed to uncovering their pure, unconditional nature. To reveal this infinite purity and reside in this state is the consummate victory for the warrior. When a warrior is inseparable from his or her true nature, the enemies of attachment and aversion will never conquer this fortress of indestructible peace.

Finding peace in this world can often seem daunting and difficult, since our disturbing emotions challenge us relentlessly, even in the most serene of places. If we can tackle and defeat these internal enemies, we will find unassailable peace, even in the midst of utter chaos. Defensive maneuvers and aggressive tactics will not be required, since the real enemies — the disturbing emotions — have been vanquished on the spot. We will secure genuine victory without firing a single shot.

CHAPTER EIGHT

Sowing Seeds and Reaping Results

The Unfailing Law of Karma

Karma refers to actions and their consequences. Our actions determine our karma by planting seeds that ripen now or at some time in the future. We must always proceed with sensitivity and care, since every thought, word, and deed has consequences and affects us as well as others. We will not act selfishly and we will be blessed with a happier life when we act in accordance with the unfailing law of karma.

It is essential to understand karma and the law of cause and effect. If you plant an apple seed, you will harvest a bushel of apples. If you place your hand near the fire, you will feel the heat. These causal relationships are obvious and easy to comprehend. In the realm of human thought and emotions, the workings of karma are less apparent and more difficult to grasp. Indeed, it is said that only a fully enlightened Buddha can understand all the subtle intricacies and workings of karma. However, we can reflect on our life experiences and understand how virtuous activities lead to happiness and unwholesome actions cause suffering. Careless and crude behavior will bring trouble sooner or later. If we are heedful of the consequences of every thought and action, we will never harm anyone.

Every footstep in the forest leaves a small mark, rustles a few leaves, and slightly shifts the soil. Much as light leaves an impression on photographic film, our every thought and action leaves an imprint on our mind stream that will remain until its karmic effects are experienced.

We always have choices, and each choice we make has consequences. If you smile at a stranger, you are likely to get a friendly response. If you confront your adversary with a clenched fist, you will receive a clenched fist, or maybe even worse! Always make an effort to be kind and considerate. Like a line of falling dominos, good actions trigger good results, so goodness proliferates. When you understand karma, you will make an effort to walk in your neighbor's shoes, so to speak, and not always insist on getting your own way.

The unfailing law of karma is indisputable. The Buddha taught us that every action has repercussions, not only in this life, but also in future lives. If you act with the assurance that positive actions yield positive consequences, it will make a difference in your life — in your family, in your community, and in your world. Unwholesome actions drag us down into suffering. If our actions are wholesome in this life, we can create positive momentum over many lifetimes that will bring us closer and closer to enlightenment.

There is a story I heard recently about a miserly man who wore only tattered clothing, begged for food, and never gave a cent to others, even though he had a steady income from his work. When he died, the villagers searched his hut, thinking they could use the money that he hoarded away to pay for his cremation and funeral. However, they were surprised when they found not a penny. Some time later, after tending to his funeral and cremating his body, the villagers went to clean up his dwelling. His bed was made of clay and bricks and under the mattress was a small, tightly fitting wooden door. Prying it open, the villagers found a huge stockpile of cash, and resting upon it was an enormous and frightening scorpion! The villagers were convinced that this stingy man had been reborn as a scorpion, grasping his precious treasure.

In this tradition, we follow a virtuous path that will bring us closer to our true nature. We attempt to refrain from unwholesome thoughts and actions, which obscure this nature. We will mature in our spiritual practice if we never forget the unerring principle of karma and are careful about what we think and how we behave. This is why the great masters often ask their students, "Do you believe in karma?" If they say they do not, the masters refuse to give them sacred teachings. When their students demonstrate understanding and conviction in the workings of karma, they bless them with the highest and most profound teachings. If you were to receive profound instruction without conviction in the nature of karma, it could inflate your ego and act like a deadly sword that kills your chances for liberation.

The selfish ego is the breeding ground for karma. Actions that are unstained by selfish motivation are pure actions and will not cause suffering for anyone. These pure actions will not create karma. When one is free of ego and seamlessly integrated with this pure, compassionate energy, one no longer creates negative or positive karma, and one no longer experiences karmic consequences. This does not mean that an enlightened being ceases to function or turns into a lifeless rock.

Upon attaining enlightenment, boundless energy manifests in spontaneous activity that is free from consequences. Enlightened action is pure and joyous, since it always emanates from a heart of compassion and concern for others. Energy flows naturally when unimpeded by ego, just as a river flows naturally when not blocked by a dam. Free from the confinement of ego, one manifests the energy of perfect compassion throughout the world, in this life and in future lives. This compassionate energy may manifest in many ways; there could be a thousand emanations in a thousand forms, in order to perfectly benefit all.

GOING AROUND IN CIRCLES

When we are controlled by our delusions and desires, we are trapped in the vicious circle of samsara and led by unwholesome habits. We are incessantly tormented by conflicting thoughts and turbulent emotions. We are constantly on the move, but we never reach our destination. It is like an endless race on a moving treadmill that only exhausts us.

Samsara is often perceived as disgusting, but this does not mean that our world is inherently impure. Lacking awareness of the nature of mind and reality, samsara manifests as impure and repulsive. We are not integrated with our experience in a healthy way.

In spite of anxiety and unrest, we prefer to think that everything is just fine. Why not gorge on delicious food? Why not sport the finest clothes? Why not engage in as much sex as we can? Why not live in a hedonistic way? However, we cannot enjoy anything fully this way, and the more we indulge, the more we want. There seems to be no escape from this unsatisfying cycle, this paradox of pleasure seeking. If samsara were not self-perpetuating, we could jump in now and then. But samsara is entanglement, and once we are in, it could be very difficult to get out.

How do we escape from this wearisome realm? How can we live without negative consequences? How can we enjoy life freely, without addiction to pleasure and attachment to the ephemeral? It is up to us to use our intelligence and liberate ourselves from the confinement and suffering of samsara. No one can do it for us. As the Buddha said, be a lamp and a refuge for yourself.

No matter how strong or powerful we appear on the surface, there is vulnerability in all of us. Be sensitive to this vulnerability, and you will feel more empathy for everyone. Seeing the vulnerability and the beauty in the eyes of others will give birth to a sympathetic heart and loosen the bonds of self-grasping. Your compassion will douse the flames of anger and hostility in others. Communication will be friendly and warm, leaving everyone feeling satisfied. You will weaken the grip of samsaric delusion. This is karma — good karma.

With the dawn of awakening, the pain and weariness of samsara will cease. We will enjoy perfect freedom and contentment, inseparable from every moment. Each moment will be totally complete. This is the beauty of awakening.

Confronting Chaos

"Courageous simplicity" could describe our first thought, and "chaotic world" could describe every thought that follows. In the spur of the moment, if our first thought is pure and complete, this fearless simplicity will take care of everything. The first thought does not have to be extremely ambitious, such as the wish to become a great spiritual being. Rather, we can just allow our intelligence to radiate as we remain in our natural state, free from elaboration. This requires courage because we need to have unequivocal trust and conviction in this basic state of simplicity.

There is no need to escape from this chaotic world, since life would be rather boring without any disorder. We are not robots; we are human beings with the gift of a brain that generates endless thoughts. Our thoughts provide endless opportunities to become stronger and develop new skills. The problem is not the chaos itself but our lack of confidence that we can deal with the chaos.

When we experience trouble in our lives, we rush to spiritual practice. However, when things are going well, we forget about meditation. We are fickle, like fair-weather friends to our true selves. But you cannot afford to be a fair-weather friend if you want to courageously face this chaotic world. We can invigorate our spiritual practice by remembering that we have this precious opportunity to practice, that life is fleeting, and that death is impending.

There may come a time in your life when you feel thoroughly exhausted and defeated by your restless thoughts and stormy emotions. If you can give it all up and let it all go, you will breathe a huge sigh of relief and relax in total ease. When you have the courage to embrace simplicity, from that moment on you will find the strength to face everything, no matter what happens. You will confront sickness, sorrow, and despair — as well as joy, success, and achievement — without any difficulty. The simple answer is merely to embrace everything. Then you will come to see all of life as an enchanting dance.

The great masters and sages of the past are known as liberators because they emancipated themselves from suffering and helped to free others. These masters were uncompromising. They developed confidence in their ability to see the world and face the world exactly as it is. We should emulate their way of being. In recognizing their source of strength, we will discover our source of strength. Facing the world as it is, we will be liberated. Courageous simplicity will be ours when we reveal it within ourselves. Then we can live simply in a chaotic world.

FINE-TUNING

Fine-tuning our behavior is how we progress toward awakening. The Buddha himself said, "Tighten, tighten, then loosen, loosen." When we are perfectly attuned, we will not need to make further adjustments. Until we reach this perfectly balanced state, we must work diligently on being completely genuine. There should be no fabrication or pretense. We should face whatever is in front of us and take it for what it is worth.

As you fine-tune your behavior, assess your progress. Are you more tolerant and caring? Are you more easygoing and amenable to change? Like a spy, you should watch yourself all the time. The moment you find yourself being irritable or disagreeable, say to yourself, "Stop it. I am not going to babysit you anymore. I have done this for lifetimes, for eons. This is enough!" You have to be self-deprecating, so to speak, until you tame your ego and master yourself.

Continually encourage yourself and be vigilant in your approach. Ask yourself, "Am I doing anything wrong?" When you encounter any subtle selfishness, fine-tune your mind by acknowledging this pettiness and feeling regret right on the spot. Our teachers taught us that negative karma does not have any good qualities. However, we can purify our negative karma when we acknowledge unwholesome actions and express sincere regret. This is the only redeeming quality of negative karma.

Always be heedful about how you behave in your life. This

does not mean that you will not continue to create karma. You do not need to tie yourself down or stiffen up — you do not have to be that serious. Just be watchful and determine whether any selfishness influences your thoughts, words, or actions. If you wish to live a carefree life, free from the causes of suffering, you should always employ discernment and understand the uselessness of your selfish ways of thinking.

CHAPTER NINE

Perfect Freedom

FREE FROM DUALITY

Thoughts and emotions are expressions of pure energy, but when we identify with our concepts and feelings, we cannot dance freely with this energy. We compulsively accept or reject whatever arises in our experience. The extremes of dualistic thinking impede a direct and spontaneous relationship with the moment. Divisive notions such as gain and loss, pleasure and pain, like and dislike, and high and low obscure the clarity of mind's pure nature. The fundamental duality is that of "I" and "other." However, when fully integrated with the moment, there is no "I" or "other" that is separate from the moment.

In the Buddhist tradition, we begin our spiritual journey by taking refuge in the *Three Jewels*.[1] Throughout our lives we are always taking refuge in something. We seek security and protection in our friends, our spouse, our job, and our home. In some ancient cultures, people took refuge in the sun and moon, or in animals, trees, and mountains. On the spiritual path, we recognize our teacher as the truly infallible source of refuge, since the teacher can guide us toward enduring happiness and freedom. For some, taking refuge in the teacher could appear dualistic, since we may view the teacher as someone higher than us, who

---

1. The Three Jewels are the Buddha, Dharma, and Sangha. One takes refuge, or seeks protection in, the Buddha, the teacher; in the Dharma, the teachings; and in the Sangha, those who follow the way of the Buddha.

possesses more wisdom and virtue than we do. However, the teacher is a reflection of our own innate wisdom. When we take refuge in the teacher, we are actually seeking protection in our own potential for awakening.[2]

The ultimate refuge is to be free from duality itself, but sometimes we have to progress gradually, like a child who slowly grows and matures. Following a path of gradual practice introduces us to the joyful realm of nonduality. The clouds of dualistic concepts vanish, and we experience pure, nondual perception.

When you relate to your life intelligently — free from extremes — you will be capable of confronting each new challenge. Regrets about the past or hopes for the future will not obscure clear seeing. You will be free from the vacillation of hope and fear. To be without hope does not mean that you will become passive and cease to engage with the world. Most of the time, hope is born from a sense of deprivation and a desire for something more. If you value your life and are content with what you have, hope will disappear. This will give way to the spirit of adventure. To be adventuresome is to be fully open and awake, with the ability to dance skillfully with every experience. You will have good dancing legs and good dancing feet.

The moon appears in various guises, sometimes radiant and full, sometimes a mere sliver of light. When the moon is completely full, you will not cling to its beauty because you know that it continuously waxes and wanes. But more than that, you will appreciate the splendor of the entire transformation. With this understanding, you are beyond hope and fear. You are beyond all dualistic extremes, which is the expression of real freedom.

---

2. The role of the teacher is discussed in chapter 14.

REMEMBER THE PERFECT MOMENT

The thought that arises in the moment does not rest on solid ground. When you recognize this, the thought dissolves effortlessly. At that time clarity and luminosity arise[3] and there is pure, empty space. What do we mean by emptiness here? Ultimately, the true nature of all phenomena is beyond any descriptive words; therefore, in truth, things are "empty" of fixed concepts. We merely impute qualities and characteristics to the things we perceive and assign them mental labels. When we understand that they have no true existence, our thoughts will not have the power to deceive or disturb us.

Discursive thought is the troublemaker because it drags us again and again into delusion and suffering. We need to be free from the limitations of thought, but we cannot free ourselves by trying to suppress thoughts. Rather, when we realize the essence of thoughts, they dissolve on their own. Like a snake untying itself, it happens naturally. This is the profundity of the Buddha's ultimate teaching, and is known as the "effortless path."

Because thoughts dissolve naturally, you do not need to apply effort. However, this does not mean that you can simply be

---

3. Here, *luminosity* refers to the clear and knowing aspect of the mind. Phenomena are said to be luminous deities, in that everything we perceive is an expression of the mind's clarity and cognitive capacity.

lazy and undisciplined. In this tradition, that is not recommended at all! People often misunderstand this teaching as an excuse for doing nothing. They fool themselves about what effortlessness means. To practice on this path, you have to be the most sensitive, organized, and diligent person. A graceful dancer who performs with ease must still practice routinely to keep her body flexible and strong. For the general practitioner, the "effortless path" still requires the effort of meditative practice. Through the discipline of meditation, conceptual understanding will blossom into direct experience. We will go beyond the intellect and directly experience the true essence of mind.

Be aware and remember to ask the question "Who is this 'I' that is experiencing?" Metaphorically speaking, use awareness as a whip to wake yourself up. The moment you feel the whip, recognize, "I am going back to this 'I' again." When you apply the whip, suddenly you are aware of the absence of "I." Spontaneously, there is freshness and pure presence!

On the relative level, we are always preoccupied with the "I" and what the "I" is experiencing. It is difficult to *remember the perfect moment*. Each moment is a perfect moment, but we just keep missing it because we keep getting lost in our mental commentaries. We get lost in samsara because we do not remember, and we lose our awareness. With pure awareness, all perceptions are perfect and complete. But we circle around and around in a whirlpool of distractions. That is what samsara is. You cannot find samsara on a street corner in New York City, because it appears in the mind. Break through samsara by working with your mind. When we are not able to break through, it is impossible to experience this perfection.

Spontaneous Fulfillment

We find much to disagree with in our lives because we have not discovered our natural perfection. When we realize this perfection, everything *is* our self, *is* our creation. Then there is beauty in both tears and laughter. There is beauty in both birth and death. Everything guides us, teaches us, and supports us. We become one with it all.

To be *one with it all* is your practice. It is not your practice to reject or accept by thinking, "This isn't good, I don't want it," or "That's a good thing, I'd like it." You abandon the duality of wanting and not wanting, and instead embrace real joy. This joy is so profound that you will not cling to it or fear its loss. You will find your inexhaustible treasure — your wish-fulfilling jewel — and you will lack nothing.

Your confidence will be strong and you will not feel impoverished. You will be spiritually rich, even if your bank account is empty. This is the view of the Great Perfection. The Great Perfection, or in Tibetan, *Dzogchen,* is the pinnacle of the Buddhist teachings — the view that the natural condition of all things is perfect, and that nothing needs to be added or taken away. It is the ultimate path for reaching direct realization of the clear and lucid nature of mind itself. It is not about perfect versus imperfect. Rather, *everything is perfect the way it is*. Everything is wonderfully self-displayed and beautifully self-organized. At this time, you are so humble and content. You do not need to attach to the view of the Great Perfection. You do not need to identify with anything. Therefore, you have everything. You are truly complete.

THE GRASS ISN'T GREENER

If we wish to experience perfect freedom, we cannot lose our connection to this present moment. Each moment is complete in itself. In this moment, perfect freedom will be ours if we embrace happiness and sorrow, pleasure and pain, *as they are*. For the most part, we cheapen this moment by habitually reliving the past, conditioning the present, and anticipating the future. There is little possibility of relating directly to this moment, and therefore no chance for complete freedom. Responding naturally and spontaneously to each moment is the ultimate freedom.

The activities of training for a marathon, preparing for a journey, or studying for an exam are not just means to an end; they are moments to be lived and experienced fully in themselves. The grass isn't greener on the other side of the fence. In one's true state, there is no next moment that is greener than this present moment! There are no exceptions, whatever your experience is. This present moment is everything.

Imagine the independence you will experience and the joy you will feel when you relate directly to this present moment. Being totally present in this moment, you will be poised if death comes in the next moment. How long we live is not the issue; it is the quality of our lives that matters. To be fully in the moment is to be your true self.

The seed of a lotus flower can remain dormant for a very long time. However, when it reaches the soil and has water and warmth, the seed will give birth to a beautiful flower. No matter how confused you have been until now, it is okay — because now is your opportunity to see clearly, to be your true self. Everyone wants to enjoy this fearless freedom. Being awakened means living freely and completely in the moment.

Nonattachment

As we go through life, we identify with our societal roles. We think of ourselves as teachers or students, leaders or followers, friends or lovers. Like actors on a stage, we play many parts, but we seldom recognize ourselves simply as breathing human beings.

As we breathe our last breaths, none of the roles we have played in life will offer comfort or security. Clinging to these limited concepts and relative conditions will cause sadness and grief. At the time of death, attachment to notions of selfhood will make it difficult to let go of our last breath, and this will cause excruciating pain.

When we are acutely aware that we are never far from our last breath, we will appreciate the worthiness and profundity of our being. This transcends the limitations of culture, race, and society. True intelligence gives us the freedom to live in this very moment, where we are not defined or limited by our roles or responsibilities. When we breathe our last breath, none of our worldly achievements or material gain will matter, so why allow ourselves to be bogged down now? Why not live freely and joyfully in this moment?

Have you ever experienced a complete breath? You may think of yourself as something special, but if you have never experienced a complete breath, are you living fully? We seldom breathe with awareness, but there is joy in breathing fully. You do not have to rush through life, achieving ambitious feats every day. No matter how much you have accomplished in life, at the time of your last breath, you will still feel you have unfinished business. The moment you breathe completely, confusion comes to a standstill and turbulence ends. In the immediacy of your breath, everything is spontaneously accomplished.

When we breathe in this way, we will not grow bored with any of the roles that we play. Instead of always fussing with the details, we will find things acceptable as they are. Disruptions will be manageable and terms will be negotiable. Breathing is an expression of life, and we will not be in conflict with anyone when we recognize that, as breathing beings, we are all equal. When we recognize that all breathing beings are our friends, we will graciously accommodate everyone. I believe that if we can breathe in this carefree way, we will have a long and happy life.

TURN TOWARD FREEDOM

Embrace freedom. Try your best not to rely on material comforts. Rather, learn how to be content by uniting with your unconditional nature. In this way, the more you challenge yourself, the more you will build confidence. On the other hand, the more attached you are to your way of living, the more reliant you will become on external conditions. When we recognize what is meaningful and worthy of our attention, we will avoid whatever burdens us, obstructs our freedom, and obscures our true nature.

From day to day our minds are changing. What pleases us today, pains us tomorrow. In our ordinary way of thinking, we want to believe that conditional circumstances are reliable and stable. However, everything we depend on and cherish soon changes and vanishes, leaving us feeling despondent and lost.

Be aware of your wants and needs, while keeping in mind the inevitability of change and the truth of impermanence. Reflect on the futility of all conditioned things. Regard all appearances as an apparition or mirage. As you move toward a mirage, you will not find any water there, only sand. Similarly, all that you experience — your youth, strength, knowledge, wealth, friendships, family, and success — are like visions in a dream or transparent rainbows in the sky. Nothing lasts forever. While you are asleep, you may dream that you are clutching a dazzling, priceless diamond, but as soon as you awaken you know that your hand is empty. When you have trust in your true, unconditional nature, your empty palm will be a testament, strengthening your confidence. Everything we cling to in this world is as insubstantial as last night's dream.

When you view appearances as dreamlike, they will neither excite nor torment you. You will see the humor in life and get the joke, so to speak. Whatever you achieve in your practice — calmness, joy, lucidity — should also be viewed as a dream. Then there is the possibility to have even greater dreams. The greatest dream is enlightenment itself. After all, enlightenment is also a dream. Paradoxically, we speak of achieving enlightenment, but there is no truly existing enlightenment to achieve.

Ultimately, the nature of your being is ineffable — you cannot express it, but you can experience it. When you experience this great dream, you may have all kinds of dreams or you may not dream anything at all. Still, no matter what you do, you will experience joy and freedom. You will not take anything too seriously or too lightly. Rather, you will always find balance. In this oasis of balance, you will experience your true nature — the source of great liberation.

WHAT IS SELF-LIBERATION?

To be self-liberated is to live thoroughly in the moment. In absolute truth, there is no "self" and no one in need of liberation, since the self is already liberated in the moment. The moment is liberated when one is fully present, free from self-absorption. Free in the moment, one finds that all stress and struggle will vanish.

We lose the present moment when we chase after something "better." However, if the moment is complete, we have everything and we are *fully accomplished in the moment.* Worldly success alone cannot satisfy us; however, a complete and uncompromising relationship with the moment can indeed bring us lasting satisfaction.

If we cannot be fully present in the moment, we will always feel deprived and incomplete. It is easy to talk about these things, but we could deceive ourselves by thinking that we have grasped the essence after hearing the words and the concepts. These words may be precious, but if we are imprisoned in a "jail of gold," we are still not free.[4] Conceptual understanding is very limited. Liberation is possible only when we can live freely, in

---

4. The "jail of gold" is a metaphor for clinging to an intellectual understanding of the Buddha's teaching without direct realization of it.

the immediacy of the present moment. We must embrace and embody this naked truth.[5]

The heart essence of every moment is very deep and vast. Ask yourself, "Do I have the courage to experience freedom from the past, freedom from the future, and even freedom from the present? Am I willing to go beyond the concept of self and others? Am I daring enough to go beyond the intellect and the emotions in order to experience this true essence?" Liberating every moment is the heart of this tradition. We practice liberating our desire, anger, envy, pride, and ignorance.

What is the basis for liberation in every moment? A conch shell is white from the beginning, and it remains white even after it is soiled with mud and buried in the earth for eons. Your innate nature is like a white conch shell — primordially pristine and perfect. When you can see this purity, everything will be spontaneously liberated in the moment. In other words, there is nothing to prevent you from being who you are, fully in this moment. Every moment of your life is a complete moment, and recognizing this completeness is the basis of self-liberation.

5. An essential aid for preserving awareness in the present moment is the practice of meditation, which is discussed in chapter 10.

NOT CLINGING TO ANY POINT OF VIEW

The masters of the Great Perfection lineage always stressed that one's worldly responsibilities and lifestyle are not of primary importance. To embrace our true essence is the main point. You do not have to acquire anything extraneous; you only need to realize the wealth that you possess within. This teaching states that one's essential nature is timelessly pure and perfect. This flawless purity does not require any fabrication, because it is self-existing and self-sustaining. Being one with this complete state is the ultimate solution for all of our troubles, the one medicine that cures every disease.

In the view of the Great Perfection, everything is perfect in its own place. If your roommate is snoring, then he's snoring — that's it. You do not need to accompany his snoring with flutes and violins. You can find the rhythm there and accept it. The snoring of your roommate could be as beautiful as a Gregorian chant. Everything has this air of inexpressible magic, and anything is possible. If you insist that it should be some other way, you are clinging to your own contrived version of reality. In the Great Perfection, there is no clinging to any point of view. If you cling to a point of view, you do not recognize or accept things as they are.

The tradition of the Great Perfection holds the utmost respect for each individual's pure, innate nature. It recognizes and acknowledges the fundamental goodness within every being. Ultimately, nothing "good" needs to be established and nothing "bad" needs to be eliminated. With respect to discovering one's innate nature, these teachings do not talk about achieving anything because you cannot construct what is unconditional and self-existing from time without beginning. Living without the ideal of progress or the notion of self-improvement is not easy, since it requires supreme trust in the self-existing perfection of things exactly as they are.

I was once asked before a teaching, "Do you prepare for your talks beforehand?" And I thought to myself, "That's a good question!" Is there any way to genuinely prepare, and if so, what would I prepare for? If I prepare something nice to say to others, I have lost my freedom and become their slave. So the answer is no, I do not feel compelled to fabricate anything. What I share with others is the kindness of my teacher and a glimpse of perfect freedom.

CHAPTER TEN

Meditation as a Way of Life

MEDITATION IS NECESSARY

It is not enough to simply study the teachings; one actually has to live them. Once we have some understanding of the teachings, we need to apply discipline and practice meditation. Most of us cannot embody these teachings overnight. We may have some conceptual understanding, but we cannot put this understanding into action right away. A novice cook cannot simply read from a recipe book and expect to cook like a master chef. One must labor in the kitchen and learn how to use the tools and combine the proper ingredients. To integrate these teachings into our lives, we need to learn the methods and practice meditation.

If you do not actualize these teachings through practice, you may be utterly defenseless when faced with challenges, like a baby in the midst of a battlefield. When you practice meditation, gradually the mind will settle into its natural state, shielded from the onslaught of disturbing thoughts and emotions. Without the discipline of meditation, it is so easy to be tricked by one's mind. Thinking we have grasped the essence of the teachings when we have merely understood the words can truly be the worst trap.

To avoid self-deception, take these teachings to heart and apply them in your life. We may think we are very clever; we all know how clever the mind can be! However, when we stop fooling ourselves, we become our own best friend. Once we have direction and focus, we will steadily come to see everything with more and more clarity.

Practice meditation in order to calm your busy mind and develop insight into the mind's true nature. Meditation is not the end of spiritual practice, but it is a powerful tool that can reveal profound wisdom. Beyond that, you should not have a preference for or against meditation. If you resist meditation or prefer not to meditate because you think meditation is boring or passive, you have become stuck in your habitual point of view. You are attached to the idea of not meditating, and so you cannot even get past the first hurdle. Whether based on fear, laziness, or ego-driven ideas of progress, your habits are dragging you down, like a weak swimmer dragged below the ocean's surface by strong undercurrents. On the spiritual battlefield you will be defenseless, and your thoughts and emotions will overwhelm you. If you cannot discipline yourself, you will lose your sense of dignity.

My advice is to treat yourself kindly — take these sacred teachings to heart. Integrate the discipline of meditation into your life. You will benefit yourself while also benefiting your colleagues, friends, and family. You may even benefit your enemies.

I encourage you to practice meditation. With conviction in the practice and some perseverance, you will experience a ceaseless stream of benefits and blessings. Making these teachings an integral part of your life will keep you completely satisfied. Please do not think that this is something unattainable, because, in reality, all of us possess the potential to actualize our true nature and free ourselves from the disturbing emotions that sabotage our peace of mind. No one, including Shakyamuni Buddha, has a monopoly on this essence. This essence is inherent within everyone. If you are diligent and devote your time and energy to practice, you will experience the liberating results.

Learning to Focus:
A Basic Meditation

It is a misunderstanding to think that the practice of meditation is merely a method for relieving stress and achieving peace for oneself alone. Begin your meditation with a generous attitude. Each time you sit down to meditate, make your practice an offering for all beings. Recognize that everyone is looking for ways to find happiness, just as you are. Meditation is a means to this end. Sustained meditation practice will bring you joy, and a joyful mind will naturally benefit others. Resolve to meditate with this unselfish attitude.

When we begin meditation, we should first learn how to focus. Some discipline is required in order to be attentive in the moment and experience it fully. Most of the time, we are unable to focus our attention and are easily distracted. Our minds wander, and we are easily mesmerized by our perceptions and thoughts. We have a difficult time remaining focused.

There are many ways to practice meditation. Let's explore one approach. Sit up straight. When you begin, breathe naturally. Slowly settle into your breathing by counting the in and out movement of your breath twenty-one times. Touch the tip of your tongue lightly to the roof of your mouth. If you become drowsy, your tongue will drop down and rouse you from your slumber. Raise your tongue to the roof of your mouth again and concentrate. If possible, sit with your legs crossed, keep your eyes open, and look straight ahead, beyond the tip of your nose. I would advise you not to close your eyes. If you were to suddenly encounter a tiger in the jungle and were overcome with fear, closing your eyes would not make the tiger run away. Similarly, when you meditate, closing your eyes will not make your distracting thoughts and feelings disappear. You will be alert and prepared to face any challenge when you keep your eyes open. You may think you can meditate more effectively with your eyes closed, but most likely, you are not meditating better, you are sleeping better.

Once you have adjusted your body and settled into your breathing, focus on a specific object, such as the form of the Buddha. This could be an actual statue or an image visualized in the mind's eye. You could select one aspect, such as the Buddha's gentle eyes or his golden color. When you notice that your mind has wandered away from its focal point, gently bring it back. If you find yourself thinking about your stock portfolio or that you forgot to turn on the dishwasher, return your attention to the Buddha's image. The value of your stock portfolio is a mundane matter and your dirty dishes can wait. The mind is running around like a restless monkey all the time. Obviously, this practice can be quite challenging. Observe how long you can hold the object of your attention without wandering. If you can hold your attention steady for five minutes, you are a great meditator already! More likely, you will lose your focus, jumping from one thought to the next, like a monkey leaping from tree to tree. Staying with the object without drifting away is very difficult; it will take all of your attention and resolve. Throughout your day, you can practice this meditation technique whenever you have some free time.

Practice meditation for whatever length of time you wish. However, in the beginning, practice for short periods, perhaps just five minutes. After meditating for five minutes, you might feel that you are struggling with your mind. If so, relax and tell yourself, "You spoiled brat, go wherever you like!" Let your mind wander as far as Paris, New York, or Shanghai. You can move your body, stretch, dance, or go a little crazy. Once you feel refreshed, return to your meditation again for five more minutes. Proceed like this — concentrating and then relaxing — for perhaps half an hour to an hour. Practice for whatever length of time you find comfortable, without overexerting yourself. Maintaining unwavering attention for five minutes is much better than getting lost in distraction for five hours.

This basic practice of focusing attention is important, even for the most advanced practitioners. If you allow a glass full of muddy water to sit undisturbed, the dirt will settle to the bottom, leaving a glass of pure water. Practicing this simple technique of focusing and restoring your attention when your mind wanders will pacify your restless thoughts. It will calm your mind, and with sustained practice, you will experience lucidity and pure presence.

When you practice meditation, the trials and tribulations — the highs and lows — of your day-to-day life will not disturb you too much, since your body and mind will be more relaxed. There will be a more intimate connection between your meditation practice and whatever comes up in your life. Even if chaotic or fearsome events turn your world upside-down, you will have more space and less stress. If your life swerves off the road and crashes, the fruits of your practice will act like an airbag, buffering you against serious injury. You will have the strength and clarity to master challenging situations.

Practice by focusing and holding your attention. If you cannot discipline yourself in this way, you could easily find yourself behaving like a spoiled and pampered child who feels helpless when confronted with a challenging situation. When you develop the capacity to be present, you will respond competently, no matter what the circumstances.

Endeavor to practice some form of meditation each day. Even if you are transacting million-dollar business deals, this will pale in comparison to the rewards of a regular meditation practice. You can live without a million-dollar deal, but you cannot live without inner peace and well-being. So be good to yourself. Make a profound deal with yourself to practice every day. Set aside a little time for meditation, and then gradually spend more and more time practicing. In this way, the truth of the teachings will unfold within the depths of your heart. If you allow these teachings to remain only in your head, you could carelessly misuse the rest of your precious human life. This is not a practice for beginners only. Everyone must master this discipline before they can proceed further in their practice.

After meditating, rejoice and dedicate the fruits of your practice to all beings. With joy, rest in a sublime state. Make this aspiration:

> *Whatever benefit I have gained from this practice, may the residual effects last for many days, years, and lifetimes. May everyone, including myself, benefit from the wisdom and clarity accumulated in this practice, until all beings attain enlightenment. Whatever merit I have gained, I dedicate it for the welfare of all sentient beings.*

By making this dedication, you will preserve this positive energy, and your practice will grow stronger in the future. You can draw on this energy for the dual benefit of yourself and others.

Practice All the Time

We have a tendency to procrastinate when it comes to spiritual practice, thinking that all of our worldly affairs come first. However, when it comes to spiritual practice, there are no categories per se — everything we do can be practice. There is nothing more important than spiritual growth, and even as you work and play, you can flavor your activities with mindfulness and contemplation. As awareness grows, even seemingly insignificant events in your life can become great teachers. Without the inspiration that comes from spiritual endeavor, life can quickly become stale, so it's best to practice all the time. That is to say, whatever you are doing, make it spiritually rewarding. For instance, reading this book can become practice.

We are always inseparable from our breath, yet most of the time we are unaware that we are breathing. While you are reading, most likely you are not conscious of your breath. While you read this book, try broadening your focus and expanding awareness beyond its pages; this will enhance and deepen your understanding.

Why do we have to be constantly occupied? Is it because we do not enjoy the fullness of our being in the movements of our breath? If we cannot appreciate the marvelous gift of breath, we might as well be dead. We could have all the wealth and entertainment we desire, but if we cannot breathe fully in the moment, we are like walking corpses.

When your mind is distracted, you do not experience its natural clarity. Even if you were fortunate enough to hear profound teachings, they would not have any real impact. Even if you were to meditate in the mountains for years, it would not change the quality of your being. In order to experience the sublime state of your being, you have to know how to be present. You will experience well-being when you are completely inseparable from the flow of each breath. When breath and life flow together as effortlessly as milk into tea, you will savor every moment:

> *You are here to enjoy this gentle breathing.*
> *You are here to enjoy this delightful walk.*
> *You are here to enjoy this restful day.*
> *You are here to enjoy this mesmerizing dance.*
> *You are here to relish this magical display.*

THE THREE SUBLIME PRACTICES

In the Buddhist tradition, there are three sublime practices:
The first sublime practice is the generation of a compassionate and loving heart, also known as pure intention. We begin each activity with the positive intention that our action will be of benefit to others.

The second sublime practice is the activity or practice itself, which we do mindfully, while remaining in the natural state, free from distraction.

The third sublime practice is the dedication of merit. Merit refers to the wholesome and positive momentum that grows from our practice. We dedicate our most precious essence and all the positive energy that we have accumulated from our practice to the welfare of all beings.[1]

Apply these three sublime practices in all of your activities, even something as simple as drinking a cup of tea. Prepare your tea while generating a compassionate heart, the pure intention to benefit all sentient beings. This is the first practice. Then drink the cup of tea with complete mindfulness. This is the second practice and the core of the three practices. After your last sip, dedicate the enjoyment of your drink for all beings, and pray that they may be liberated from suffering and awaken to enlightenment.

---

1. The accumulation of merit is discussed in more detail in chapter 11.

The rays of the sun provide warmth for all creatures without discrimination. We dedicate the virtue of every positive action to the benefit of all beings. In this tradition, we do not hold on to the merit that we have accumulated for our own benefit alone, but instead we dedicate this positive energy so that someday the enlightened qualities of every being will manifest. Finally, the perfect dedication is to dissolve your merit in the unconditional state.

In this way, simply drinking a cup of tea becomes genuine meditation because of the three sublime practices. Always insure that these three practices are inseparable from whatever you do. The first and last are quite straightforward. In the case of the second sublime practice, you have a specific target. For instance, if your activity is meditation on the breath, follow your breath attentively, and at the same time be mindful of its ephemeral quality. The three sublime practices are the best way to elevate your thinking and walk with dignity on the path of awakening.

BREATHING MEDITATION:
HELLO AND GOODBYE

S it with your back erect and look straight ahead with your eyes wide open. Inhale and exhale. Do not force your breathing or try to modify it in any way. Do not think of yourself as the one who inhales or exhales. Just be with your breath, naturally and sincerely.

Recognize and watch your breath. When you inhale, recognize the inhalation, and when you exhale, recognize the exhalation. Be present in the breath. When inhaling, welcome the breath by saying silently in your mind, "Hello." When exhaling, bid farewell to the breath by saying, "Goodbye."

With every inhalation and exhalation, repeat, "Hello, goodbye, hello, goodbye." In this practice, you are neither rejecting nor accepting what comes and goes. When the breath comes in, you welcome it with awareness; when the breath goes out, you bid farewell by mindfully letting it go. Try not to miss a single inhalation or a single exhalation. When you do this practice, do not let anything distract you. Maintain fresh awareness of your breath.

You might be wondering, What is the purpose of saying, "Hello and goodbye"? Actually, this practice has no purpose. The practice of hello and goodbye has always been our natural way, but at some point we were diverted. We became lost and bewildered, and frustration and suffering grew.

To be free of confusion and suffering, we have to return to

our primary purpose, which is this basic practice of hello and goodbye. Hello and goodbye is all we need. We accumulate so many things, but the more we accumulate, the more we suffer. There is no good reason for collecting so many things. Embrace the way that has existed from time immemorial, which is to say, "Hello and goodbye." There is no need to worry, even if you recently got divorced or lost your job. You no longer have to dwell on these things because your practice is simply to say, "Hello and goodbye."

This practice allows you to simply be yourself and see reality just as it is. You recognize your essence when you say, "Hello." Your essence is like space; it is wide open and easily accommodates your thoughts, feelings, and perceptions. Like a vast ocean, you welcome everything that swims through your open expanse.

You acknowledge your unobstructed nature when you say, "Goodbye." Appearances arise without beginning or end, but you cannot grasp or hold on to any aspect of this unceasing display. You cheerfully bid farewell to every passing appearance.

It is like watching a beautiful bubble arising from water. You welcome it with "Hello." Immediately the bubble bursts, and as it does, you say, "Goodbye." There is no anticipation because you are not looking forward and no regret because you are not looking back. Without any reference to past or future, there is only the eternal present — and that is to say, "Hello and goodbye."

Nonmeditation Is
the Ultimate Meditation

The goal of our practice is to free ourselves from stress and suffering. We cannot actualize this freedom using a purely intellectual approach. We need to experience these teachings directly and embody them in our lives. This is why I strongly recommend the practice of meditation.

As beginners, we must embrace the practice of meditation. Even if the discipline of meditation does not come easily, we should endeavor to practice. We have to tame our neuroses and pacify our restless minds.

Steady discipline, combined with joyful effort, is the best way to respect and care for yourself. As your practice progresses, you will begin to reap the rewards. You will carry yourself in a majestic way and experience the regal qualities of your wakeful nature. Like a king in command of his subjects, you will master your mind and emotions.

Every moment is a new moment, so we need a fresh approach to meditation that can be practiced by everyone, anywhere in the world. Our meditation will be pristine when we recollect, with an open heart, the basic goodness in all beings. There is no time to be narrow-minded or territorial, as life is too precious to waste. We should not spoil a single moment with an unwholesome thought. This dynamic form of meditation can be practiced nonstop, so that living itself becomes meditation.

Moment-to-moment awareness is the supreme form of meditation. All other methods of meditation are steps that lead us toward this all-pervasive awareness. Recognizing the essence of one's mind and learning to remain in this essence is true meditation. In Tibetan, *meditation* means "getting used to." We could say that meditation is not the goal, but a tool that helps us discover or "get used to" the true nature of mind. Once you realize the truth, you no longer need the tool. When resting in the mind's nature, there is nothing left to meditate on because the mind is no longer distracted! There is nothing more to grow accustomed to. Nonmeditation is the ultimate meditation. Whatever comes, you are capable of handling it because everything is self-liberated as it arises.

If you must have a quiet and secluded place to meditate, your practice is still ordinary. However, with moment-to-moment awareness we can manage any situation. This is what we need the most because life is often chaotic and challenging. We have to survive and navigate the strains and stresses of everyday life. Buddhist practice is not simply a matter of reciting mantras, chanting prayers, and quietly meditating. True practice means learning to handle every situation skillfully.

Whatever you are doing, do it comfortably. Proceed in a relaxed and natural manner. You will experience thoughts arising one after the other. A thought comes and it goes. When you are alert and aware, you will not get lost in your thoughts. It will be clear that you are not your thoughts and that your thoughts do not define you. Thoughts are like the flight of a bird through the sky: the path of the bird leaves no trace. Each thought has no dwelling place or destination. When you train this way, the "possessor" of these thoughts will eventually disappear. At this point, there will be no one to suffer or experience any torment. This is moment-to-moment awareness and the perfection of nonmeditation.

CHAPTER ELEVEN

Practicing on the Path

Nothing Is Working

From the beginning we should ask ourselves, "How free am I from wrongful thinking and harmful actions?" We should readily acknowledge our faults and weaknesses. We should accept the fact that we need to work on ourselves, that our attitudes and conduct need some adjustment. Following a spiritual path requires the courage to remain alone and examine our shortcomings, free from the distraction of cell phones, chat rooms, and movies-on-demand. We need to remain alone with our thoughts and confront ourselves just as we are, without any diversions.

The best way to begin our practice is to recognize that nothing is working. As time moves on, our plans fall apart and we lose the things that we cherish most. Everything eventually fails us: our beliefs, our hopes, our vitality, and our health. We are vulnerable, and the security we hang on to is fragile. When we confront and accept this uncertainty and lack of control, we will practice meditation with greater force and conviction.

In his youth, the Buddha was known as the Prince Siddhartha. At that time, he rode his chariot outside the walls of his palace and witnessed the stark reality of human suffering. As a prince, he lived a luxurious life, surrounded by the most sumptuous pleasures, but when he saw sickness, old age, and death, he was jolted by the fact that these were his fate as well. He understood that his youth and enjoyments would eventually betray him. He recognized that attachment to earthly pleasures and security would inevitably result in bitter disappointment. He asked himself, "What is happening here? What is the purpose of life?" He realized that all conditional things were ultimately without essence. He understood that nothing was working. With heartfelt renunciation, he embarked on a path of inner discovery.

These days, meditation has become fashionable — a way for privileged people to attend special events, consume good food, interact with like-minded people, and have their picture taken with a famous Buddhist lama. Obviously, this is not genuine practice. True meditation will heighten your sensitivity and sharpen your insight. You will see more clearly everyone's deepest desires and most difficult suffering. If you think you are special simply because you meditate, you are being a little arrogant. After all, spiritual practice is not a way to bolster your ego or show off. Genuine practitioners of meditation are never pretentious; instead, they embody real humility and sincere concern for others.

An accomplished meditator is capable of overcoming every obstacle in life. Developing this level of confidence requires an approach that goes beyond simply resting in a state of repose. It is not sufficient to learn a few techniques and practice meditation just to relax and quiet your mind. To sit calmly in your room, still your thoughts, and drift into a state of torpidity is not meditation. A cow may sit still and breathe quietly when its stomach is full, but can we call this meditation?

Meditation is not just for relaxation; its primary purpose is to develop the capacity to respond skillfully and gracefully to life's difficulties as well as its joys. We have to reflect deeply on the uncertainty and brevity of our lifespan. Contemplate the fact that all the things in which we place our trust are contingent and constantly changing. We have to use our spiritual practice to look within and discover the heart of our being.

Followers of the spiritual path must proceed in this way. Only then will we have the opportunity to experience the real essence and value of our human life. It is our chance to be reawakened, our precious opportunity to enjoy boundless energy and employ consummate skill for our own well-being and for the well-being of others.

This Is a Fantasy

We often find it difficult to discipline ourselves and practice the Dharma[1] when we are happy. It is easy to forget about spiritual endeavor when our lives are running smoothly. In order to motivate ourselves, we should contemplate the suffering we invariably experience when driven by selfish desires. To intensify our awareness of impermanence, we should visualize ourselves in hellish realms and imagine fearful experiences that are very different from what we know now.

Right now we are living in a fantasy. We like to believe that death is not a possibility for us if we are young or healthy. But the clock is ticking, and as we say in Tibet, the lord of death is always waiting at the doorstep. Imagine yourself with nothing to eat or nowhere to take shelter. Envision the terror of being caught in a tsunami or a war zone. Train yourself in this way to honestly confront and contemplate the realities of suffering and change.

To face reality in this way, you do not have to seek out famous lamas or perform exotic spiritual rituals. I often tell my friends not to think about practicing meditation or chasing after lamas. If you must, first enjoy what the world has to offer. Make sure you do not leave anything out. Sooner or later, there will

---

1. *Dharma* is a Sanskrit word that in this context means the teachings of the Buddha and the practices that lead to awakening.

come a time when you say, "This is enough — I have experienced every pleasure, but I have not found any fulfillment." You must go through this ordinary door first. You have to experience the pleasures of this life and see for yourself that they are ultimately unfulfilling. Only then will you be able to close this door behind you.

My own dear mother was born into a well-to-do family in Tibet, and for some time she led a comfortable life. She was an only daughter, so she was well loved and cared for and had all the things she desired. But her first marriage, to my father, did not last long. She married again and had more children, but her marriage with my stepfather was not successful and eventually he passed away, leaving my mother to take care of us all. Finally, she met a man whom she cared for deeply, and she felt that he was the love of her life. Tragically, she was not able to enjoy life with him for very long, as he passed away suddenly. Within a period of four months she lost her lover, her father, and her youngest son. Wearied and deeply saddened, she felt little desire for the things of this life. She sought out a Buddhist master, spoke of her heartbreaking experience, and expressed her wish to pursue the spiritual path. He told her that she had successfully completed half of her spiritual journey by tasting the bitter fruits of this world and feeling strong renunciation. She took ordination and became a nun, fully devoting her life to spiritual endeavor. Without the guidance and perspective that a spiritual life provides, I believe she may have lost her way, overwhelmed with pain and disappointment.

Just as you savor food when you haven't eaten for days, you will embrace the teachings of the Buddha after experiencing disillusionment with what the material world has to offer. Before the

Buddha's quest for enlightenment, he had every luxury and experienced every enjoyment, yet he felt empty and unfulfilled. He was determined to discover what is true and everlasting. He confronted the vicissitudes of life and traveled a path with honesty and sincerity, revealing the heart and the essence of his being. This is why the Buddha's teachings still resonate with us today and touch our hearts so deeply.

To Follow the Buddha

Why do we seem to be constantly restless, perpetually seeking, never satisfied? When we are twelve years old, we long to be eighteen, and when we reach eighteen, we yearn to be twenty-one. When we turn sixty, we wish we were eighteen again. It does not have to be this way. Ultimately, there is no compelling destination to reach and no lasting accomplishment to claim. We can experience something truly worthwhile without always seeking for something more.

It is senseless to continue chasing after the things that have failed us in the past. It is far more reasonable to accept life *as it is*. This is a beautiful way of living. We do not need to alter anything, and we do not need to burden ourselves, endlessly pursuing something finer. Always yearning for something else will never ensure true pleasure or satisfaction; it only stimulates more and more restlessness and desire.

Look at yourself sincerely and face up to your weaknesses. Constantly hammer away at your failings, all your clever posturing and selfish thinking. To travel this path is to mature in your understanding and grow rich in wisdom. Following this teaching does not mean simply having a statue of the Buddha in your living room and calling yourself a Buddhist. Following the Buddhist path means having a pure heart and sincere regard for others.

In other words, to follow the spiritual path means to work at becoming the Buddha. To follow the Buddha, you do not have to recite all the Buddhist mantras or learn all the Buddhist scriptures. Rather, you need to transform a narrow heart into a compassionate heart.

YOUR HIGHEST STANDARD

Will selfish ways of thinking ever lead to true joy and equanimity? Like a thief who steals from others, in the end we will feel only remorseful and wracked with guilt. If we steer our course with the decency of pure and benevolent intentions, we will never get lost in bleak and fearsome realms. If we proceed wisely, true contentment is a realistic goal that is well within our reach in this very lifetime.

Why should we begin every activity with benevolent intentions? Simply put, there is no promising alternative. We have tried everything else and found it to be counterproductive. Can selfish thinking ever serve as the foundation for future happiness? Selfishness always comes with a hefty price tag, and we have to endure the undesirable consequences. The gratification that comes from self-centered activity is conditional, and everything conditional will eventually disintegrate, like snow melting on the ground when the sun comes out.

We all experience doubt, fear, and weakness. We can be understanding and tolerant of others, even when they treat us badly. We are all doing our best to survive. Everyone is troubled by the stormy waves of desire, anger, greed, envy, and pride. We are full of these disturbing emotions! No one wishes to suffer, so why would we want to compound the misery of others?

No one deserves our harsh judgment or our condemnation.

Everyone can gain from our warmhearted support. If we hold ourselves up to this standard, we will live our lives ever more fully. When we look into each other's eyes, we can sense our shared vulnerability. We do not need to outsmart anyone, as we will all face sickness, old age, and inevitable death. Let us strive to develop all-embracing concern for others and take their trials to heart. To be compassionate does not mean that we are superior to or more virtuous than others. Such misguided, self-righteous thinking will only torment us. Compassion is simply the natural expression of a pure and noble heart. Make this your natural way, and you will enjoy the highest standard of living.

Coming and Going

The nature of mind is unobstructed. Moment by moment, one thought is born, while another one dies. This energy is unceasing, and it springs from primordial wisdom. This energy is the essence of what we are. This essence manifests, but not in any solid or substantial way. We cannot imagine it or express it. It transcends imagination and expression.

This essence is the compassionate nature of mind. From this compassionate nature, energy flows without obstruction, coming and going. We should understand that thoughts have no place to arise, no place to remain, and no place to go. They just come from vast space and disappear into vast space.

The energy of thought is unceasing. Nothing can obstruct it. No one can stop it, and yet we try. If we try to stop the unstoppable, we develop psychological problems. We are not being realistic. Thoughts are coming and going, so you do not have to try to stop them. You can simply rest in this continuum of awareness without trying to stop thoughts or let go of thoughts.

Nothing is concrete or substantial, and while everything appears in the mind, there is nothing to grasp. Do not try to conceive of it. It is like the reflections in a mirror. The mirror reflects naturally, without effort. Images just appear and disappear in the mirror. In the same way, thoughts arise and vanish in the state of mind that is ineffable and beyond words.

The mirror's potential to reflect is infinite. When there is nothing reflected in the mirror, the mirror has not lost its reflective potential. Do not think that the mirror must always reflect something. Just as the essence of our being is independent of causes and conditions, the mirror's potential to reflect is independent of the presence of an object. In other words, you can be a spiritual practitioner all the time. When there are reflections in the mirror, you can practice. When there are no reflections in the mirror, you can practice. The potential that exists in the mirror exists within you — you are the mirror.

Just watch your thoughts, like an old man watching a child at play. The child is engrossed in her games, but the old man takes none of it seriously. He is wise enough to understand that her games are flights of fancy, only the play of the mind. Thoughts are coming and going — just recognize that and remain in the continuum of mindfulness.

POINT YOUR FINGER INWARD

It is easy to point our finger at others. It is more challenging to point inward, at ourselves. It takes courage and resolve. When you point your finger inward and expose your own faults, you are a genuine human being.

When you find fault in others, the fault is often within you. When you recognize good qualities in others, it is likely a reflection of your own virtues. If our innate nature is pure and perfect, the world we reflect should be pure and perfect. If we see imperfection, our vision is obscured. We cannot see the sun when the sky is overcast. Our vision is clouded, but the sun is still shining brightly.

The best approach is to focus on your own faults. When you condemn others for their shortcomings, think, "This must be my fault. I am causing suffering for myself by being judgmental. I am rejecting what I don't like and accepting what I like. I will become bound in an endless cycle of rejecting and accepting."

Always be sure to point inward. We learn nothing when we criticize others; we learn much when we scrutinize ourselves. You will be a more tolerant person and you will have a more joyous life when you are not so quick to judge others.

When we engage in criticism and fault finding, we just bolster our egos. But ego is not like a massive boulder in the heart that needs to be forcefully extracted. In truth, ego has no tangible existence. It is actually the most fragile and vulnerable thing on earth, and that is why ego feels so insecure. We should understand the weakness of ego, and we should be confident that we could survive quite well without it.

On the other hand, ego can be very tricky and will fabricate all kinds of fixed views. For instance, have you ever felt betrayed by a friend? If you examine the thought "I have been betrayed," the "I" plays a major role. The "I" creates the concept of "friend." You define this person as your friend, and you become attached to the concept. You feel closer to your friend than you do to others, so there is bias from the start. This bias is your creation.

We can apply our intelligence to recognize when we are being tricked. There is a difference between being intelligent and being clever. When you are clever, you do not see the whole picture and you get caught up in small things. In contrast, intelligence sees the complete picture. Intelligently, you can perceive that you are solidifying your concept of friend. When you point your finger inward, there is the possibility for genuine friendship. Friendship should be formed with this kind of clear discernment and not be based solely on your own needs or expectations.

Once a student of mine — who was a lawyer — told me that his profession was not a noble one, so he would not make a good Buddhist. I did not agree. I told him that a lawyer could be an excellent practitioner on this path. If lawyers are tempted to behave unethically, this is an opportunity for them to examine their behavior and improve their character. In the same way, if you do not challenge yourself, like an athlete training to run faster and jump higher, you will never grow stronger. Having faults is not the problem. Believing you are faultless is a big problem.

There was a monk who was a very sincere and ascetic practitioner. He was scholarly and had great understanding. He lived in a monastery with eight hundred monks. The Buddha's teachings went straight to his heart, engendering compassion, kindness, and humility. He never cared to sit on a high throne or be a leader of any kind. He always sat in the last row and took a small portion of what was left to eat. But one day, a patron came to the monastery with buckets of yogurt to offer the monks. The patron began serving yogurt to the monks in the first row, filling their large bowls. This monk enjoyed yogurt very much and grew concerned as he thought to himself, "He's giving them so much yogurt, when he reaches my row, there may not be any left for me." When the patron reached the last row, the monk could see that there was still plenty of yogurt in the bucket. The patron went to put a serving into the monk's bowl, but this monk immediately turned his bowl upside down. The surprised patron asked, "What's wrong?" The monk replied, "This greedy monk already had his yogurt when you were serving the front row. He doesn't deserve any more."

Even if you were an ascetic monk — practicing meditation in a cave for years with little food and water — it would mean nothing if you were not willing to point your finger inward. If you do not acknowledge and rectify your own faults, how will you tame your ego?

ACCUMULATING MERIT AND WISDOM

In the Buddhist tradition, we accumulate merit and wisdom as the means to purify our negativity and clear away the mental fog that obscures the mind's innate clarity. We practice what are known as the *six perfections:* generosity, discipline, patience, diligence, meditation, and wisdom. Merit is accumulated when practicing the first five perfections. With the sixth perfection, one actualizes wisdom by recognizing and resting in the pure nature of mind.

When practicing the first perfection of generosity, merit is accumulated by making offerings to the teacher, to the teachings, and to those who are practicing on a spiritual path. The merit of generosity also comes from assisting the poor, the sick, and the handicapped, giving them food, clothing, protection, and shelter. With activities like these we accumulate merit. We should not pretend to be generous. There should be sincere concern for the plight of others and some sacrifice on our part. The profound practice of generosity could easily become an empty gesture, lacking the spirit of genuine caring.

Wisdom brings the practices of generosity, discipline, patience, diligence, and meditation to perfection. For example, the one who practices generosity experiences inner richness. However, there is nothing in the expression of generosity that is tangible or concrete. There is nothing you can grasp and hold on to. The real act of generosity is "empty" of a truly existing giver and receiver. Wisdom is the realization of the empty nature of all things.

Even when you realize the absolute nature of emptiness, you should not abandon the gathering of merit through the relative acts of generosity, discipline, patience, diligence, and meditation. Although you realize that in the ultimate essence there are no merits to gather, in the relative world everything is interdependent. We cannot remain in the absolute nature all of the time until we reach full enlightenment. We can, however, function in the relative world while maintaining the view of the ultimate nature of all things.

Padmasambhava, the great master who introduced the lineage of the Great Perfection into Tibet, said, "Even if your view is as high as the sky, your observance of appropriate behavior should be as fine as flour." In other words, even when we have realized the view of emptiness, the ultimate nature of things, we must always be meticulous in our actions. We should never forget the inescapable law of karma and should be keenly aware of how our actions affect others. In this sophisticated way, we will conform to the reality of interdependence.

A Savings Account for All Beings

When we apply the teachings of the Buddha and practice diligently, we develop the positive energy that we call *merit*. All virtuous activity creates vast stores of merit, which propels our spiritual growth. However, we do not hold on to the merit we have accumulated through our practice. We do not deposit it in private savings accounts and use it only for ourselves. The benefits of our practice should be readily available for everyone to draw on, a collective fund for all beings. We put our merit in a charitable account with everyone's name on it. In the Buddhist tradition, we call this the practice of *dedication*.

Not hoarding our spiritual accomplishment with pride or self-interest, we practice true generosity. We dedicate our merit for the good of all beings, and we are inspired to go further. Continually, we can offer all our clarity, insight, and wisdom for the benefit and support of others.

When we dedicate our merit properly, it will never be lost. If we do not dedicate our merit, it will eventually be exhausted. If we succumb to anger, the merit we have accumulated can be lost in an instant, as quickly as a drop of water evaporating on a hot stove. If we dedicate the merit for the welfare of others, it is like putting a drop of water in the ocean — it will never dry up.

If your accumulated merit is invested wisely on behalf of all beings, they can always share in the benefits of your practice, until everyone reaches enlightenment. If you do not dedicate your merit for the sake of all beings, you could easily become attached to whatever you achieve in your spiritual practice. You could cling to your own small world of peace and contentment. It is not sufficient to achieve happiness for oneself alone. In our Tibetan tradition, we say that if you want to have a really delicious meal, share it with someone else.

When you dedicate your merit, do not be too pleased with yourself, since in truth, there is nothing substantial to cling to. Do not hold on to your virtue, but offer it freely and joyfully. You are not trying to feed or protect your ego, since you have given everything away to others. You seal your dedication by resting in the ultimate state of emptiness, free from all attachment. This natural state of emptiness is the wish-fulfilling jewel, an unlimited reservoir of blessings for all.

CHAPTER TWELVE

The Compassionate Heart

The Four Boundless Qualities

In the Buddhist tradition, we practice developing the *four boundless qualities* of impartiality, love, compassion, and sympathetic joy. These four qualities are boundless because they are directed toward infinite sentient beings; the suffering of beings is inexhaustible, and the benefit of meditating on these qualities is immeasurable.

IMPARTIALITY

When meditating on these four boundless qualities, it is helpful to begin with the *boundless quality of impartiality*. If we cannot regard others in an even-handed way, the three remaining qualities of love, compassion, and sympathetic joy will lack a strong foundation and will not be complete.

We meet so many different kinds of people, and we tend to view them through the lens of our personal biases. We do not feel kindly toward those who treat us with indifference or cause us harm. We feel affection only for those who are kind to us, or further our interests in some way. Those we like, we tend to help. Those we dislike, we often harm. However, with this practice, we begin by viewing others impartially. We broaden our outlook and regard everyone equally.

The Tibetan word for impartiality is *tang nyom*. *Tang* means to let go of attachments and bias. *Nyom* means to make equal. *Tang nyom* means to relate to everything evenly. Can we view all beings impartially? All living beings breathe, and your friend's breath is no different from your enemy's. Breath is breath. If you meditate on this simple yet profound truth, you will have respect for everyone. On the surface, human beings appear very different from one another. However, our deepest aspirations are aligned, and the essence of our being is beyond distinctions. Know that in your essential nature you are not different from others, and then no one will feel like a stranger to you. Everyone you meet will feel like a friend.

Just as everyone breathes, everyone possesses innate intelligence. Your friend is no more intelligent than your foe. Are you going to accept your friend and reject your enemy? In that case, you are accepting only one-half of yourself. To be a complete human being, you need to accept everyone equally.

You will find no imperfection in a perfect circle and no blemish on a flawless surface. And, search though you may, you will not find a trace of bias in the kind and compassionate heart. We all possess intelligence, so it is up to us. We can do it. We can apply these teachings and we can travel this path. These teachings have been practiced for over 2,600 years, from the Shakyamuni Buddha's time until the present. Utilizing our intelligence to free ourselves of prejudice, we can reveal the profound qualities of loving kindness and compassion.

Prince Siddhartha left the security of his palace, determined to benefit all beings. How could he care for the whole world when bound by an oath to defend his own kingdom? He embarked on a quest for something far greater. His great aspiration and steadfast commitment were to relieve the suffering of all beings and guide them to perfect happiness. With the clarity of his wisdom, he viewed everyone equally. And now, because of the Buddha's realization and enlightened experience, we are able to enjoy his precious legacy. Inspired by his example, we can realize and share this sacred wisdom with everyone.

The Buddha did not strive for enlightenment in order to gain something for himself alone. His action was selfless. When we are selfless, we are Buddhas. We can trust in our innate goodness and live a joyful life, with care and understanding for others.

LOVE

The nature of all things is interdependent, and all beings are intimately connected. Directly or indirectly, all beings support us on our journey through life. Everyone deserves our kindness, and everyone is in absolute need of our care. As a mother cares for her child, we can care for everyone. This is the *boundless quality of love*.

We are all wandering in this world, tormented by the stresses and strains of daily life, and searching for ways to find happiness. Due to spiritual immaturity and persistent confusion, we are like helpless children in need of a mother's love and guidance. A mother will instinctively care for and protect her children, knowing that they are vulnerable and unable to look after themselves. No matter how badly a child behaves, a mother will be patient. Her only wish is for the happiness and well-being of her child. If you nurture and care for others with the affection that a mother has for her only child, you will feel that there is nothing flowing through your veins but love.

With broad understanding and an impartial view, you will not grow overly attached to your friends, nor will you shut out your enemies. With sincere concern for the happiness of others, your love will not be tainted with selfish attachment, so it will not become a source of pain. Ordinary love, stained with possessiveness, inevitably leads to suffering. Sooner or later, this partial love will fade, leaving you feeling lost and alone.

The first step is to learn to love yourself. Know in your heart that you are deserving of love and care. If you cannot love yourself, how can you love others? When you do not care for yourself, an essential ingredient is missing, and it is difficult to connect with others. First, reestablish the connection by nurturing your innate nature. Then, genuine regard for others will reignite your passion for life. Love is the best medicine for all negativity and harm, so love yourself, and then love all beings.

COMPASSION

One might ask, What is the difference between love and compassion? We used the example of the care that a mother has for her child to describe the boundless quality of love. The metaphor of the butcher illustrates the *boundless quality of compassion.*

If you were to witness a butcher sharpening his blade, preparing to slaughter a sheep right before your eyes, how would you feel? You would feel unbearable sorrow for the suffering that this innocent creature was about to endure. The boundless quality of compassion is the visceral feeling of concern for the pain and suffering of others.

Metaphorically speaking, the butcher is everywhere. He is standing in our pathway. We are suffering because this butcher is killing us, draining the lifeblood of our freedom and joy, and robbing us of our precious time. This butcher is our afflictive emotions. Everyone suffers from the pains of desire, anger, envy, greed, and pride. These insidious emotions steal away our peace of mind. No one is immune.

We all yearn for serenity and joy in our lives. How can we help to relieve the heartache of others and rescue them from the butcher's lethal blade? A clear and profound understanding of how we all suffer gives birth to genuine compassion. We must be sensitive to the pain and frustration that everyone endures. There is not a single being who is unworthy of our compassion.

SYMPATHETIC JOY

How do we practice the *boundless quality of sympathetic joy?* Start by reminding yourself that everyone, without exception, aspires to live a happy life, free from hardship. Then, imagine that your neighbor is living in a house more grand and luxurious than yours. Many exciting things are happening there — lively parties with beautiful and sophisticated guests. Instead of feeling envious or resentful, think, "It's wonderful that my neighbor has a magnificent home and such a successful life. May she enjoy more and more happiness! May she have more satisfaction and more success in the future!" Rejoicing in the happiness of others is the practice of sympathetic joy, and with this magnanimous view, you will see the beauty of life.

Envy is the opposite of sympathetic joy. When we covet or resent what others have, we create ill will and subvert our own chances for happiness. Therefore, always be watchful for envious thoughts, and purify this negativity by feeling joy for others.

You will find countless opportunities to rejoice in the success, happiness, and good fortune of others. Rejoicing in the happiness of others will make you happy. Take pleasure in the happiness of others, and your own joy will grow beyond measure.

HOW TO MEDITATE
ON THE FOUR BOUNDLESS QUALITIES

In the Buddhist tradition, there are many ways to meditate. One method is the pacification of discursive thought through mindfulness of breath. Another approach is the use of guided contemplation, meditating on the nature of love, compassion, sympathetic joy, and impartiality. One can use this method during formal practice or in the midst of one's daily activities.

Meditate on the four boundless qualities until your heart is imbued with constant love and compassion for all. First, look upon others impartially, remembering that just like yourself, everyone desires happiness and does not want to suffer. Fortified with this understanding, make it your wish that all beings be as happy as you want to be. Aspire to protect them from all of the sufferings that you want to avoid. Finally, do not give in to thoughts of malice or envy. Feel joyful about the success and happiness of others.

Having this broad-minded and magnanimous view may seem unattainable. Do not be disheartened. Reflecting on these qualities for even a brief time can create positive impressions in the mind, slowly transform your mental attitude, and have a positive effect on others. In Buddhist practice, we do not cultivate these qualities for a few days, months, or years. Rather, we meditate on them throughout the course of our lives. Thus, our entire life becomes practice.

Throughout your day, meditate on love, compassion, sympathetic joy, and impartiality. At night, sleep with these four qualities in your heart. These sublime qualities will flow in an unbroken stream, and you will experience something truly meaningful. When you first hear of these teachings, you might feel uplifted and inspired, but you are getting just a glimpse — a taste of something profound. You can carry this inspiration forward and continue to reflect. As these boundless qualities unfold within your heart, you will touch the inner core of your humanity, your essence. This is a real possibility, so use your time wisely and actualize your true potential.

A Pure Heart

Always remember to be kind. Do not allow yourself to think negatively about anyone. Have a kind heart, even for those who hurt you. Remember that they act out of ignorance. Understand their suffering and confusion the way a physician understands the causes of an illness. Do not resort to aggression or confrontation. Take an interest in the lives of others. Try to elevate them and free them from distress.

When attacked with arrows, the Buddha taught us to respond with flowers. Flowers represent the beauty of compassion. When confronted with harsh or harmful behavior, we do not have to answer with aggression. Everyone deserves to be treated kindly because everyone possesses buddha nature. Remaining confident in this understanding, one is a true follower of the compassionate Buddha.

If you treat yourself with the highest respect, even your willful ego will surrender to your wakeful nature. The cunning and deceitful ego will find no opportunity to lead you astray. Instead, using your natural intelligence, you will automatically abandon your self-centered ways. Then the willful ego will not be so difficult to handle.

With a heart of compassion, every day of your life will be joyful, and your joy will be expressed in your words and gestures. With sympathetic concern, you will experience relationships fully, and you will never feel that you are better than others or that others are better than you. You will embrace all beings and secure a place for them in your heart. You will not antagonize or overwhelm others, and you will always be flexible. Like the warming fire of an open hearth, a beauty that is everlasting will radiate from within.

The more you understand yourself, the less you will deceive yourself. The more caring you are, the less confused you will be. Evaluate your own progress: Are you able to embrace others, or are you hiding out, remaining closed and narrow-minded? The more open you are, the more relaxed you will feel.

You do not have to go searching for the elephant when you find him in your own home. There is no need to go into the jungle, looking for his footprints. The elephant represents the quiet dignity of the compassionate view. The elephant is your pure heart, and your pure heart is intrinsic to your being. You do not need to go searching outside for this pure heart because it timelessly abides within you. Profound, spontaneous wisdom is nothing but the expression of this compassionate heart.

Birth of the Compassionate Heart

The compassionate heart is unconditional; therefore, it is self-liberating. If you claim ownership of this compassion, you thwart self-liberation. The problem lies in trying to grasp and hold on to things. We rarely perceive the resplendent beauty in the forms, sounds, and textures of our phenomenal world. Instead, we pigeonhole everything and live in a conceptualized, one-dimensional world. But we are not living completely if we do not experience the fullness that emanates from this compassionate heart — this unconditional heart.

You may meet brilliant spiritual teachers and contemplate profound teachings, but you will never experience ultimate fulfillment if you cannot give birth to a compassionate heart. We need to give birth to the view that frees us from bias and judgment. The teacher can help ignite your compassionate understanding. Like a shepherd leading his flock to greener pastures, the kindest teacher guides you and shows you how to take care of your heart. In a sense, this heart is not located inside or outside of you. This heart is everywhere, and everything is this heart. From time to time, stop and examine yourself. Ask yourself, "Am I able to care for myself and all beings equally, with the same pure quality of compassion? Have I given birth to a compassionate heart?"

The Profound Meaning of Compassion

In our practice, when we generate compassion, selfish thinking has no ground in which to take root and grow. Obscurations diminish, and our innate nature, open and spacious, is revealed. In this way, the essence of compassion has a very deep meaning in the Buddhist tradition. Through the generation of compassion, we bring to light the selfless, unconditional nature of our being. In Buddhism, we refer to this nature as emptiness, or in Sanskrit, *shunyata*. What does emptiness mean in this context? Emptiness refers to the ultimate nature of mind and reality, free from all relative conditions.

As we contemplate and meditate, we will slowly uncover the unconditional state that is inseparable from the essence of compassion. This is the most excellent and essential practice. With this practice alone, we can achieve liberation. Without it, we are not likely to achieve anything meaningful or enduring. We may practice many forms of meditation, yoga, and rituals, but if we do not give birth to a compassionate heart — beyond all conditional boundaries and limitations — we will have no way to achieve the ultimate fruition.

Everyone is deserving of our compassion because, ultimately, we are all interested in happiness and in freeing ourselves from suffering. All beings wish to live their lives fully. Do you feel compassion for others? Are you concerned for others, even those who dislike you or wish to do you harm? The more compassion you have for others, the happier you will be. You will be able to live on very little because your life will be very full.

Selfishness is the cause of suffering. Unselfish living results in a happy and fulfilling life. If you truly care for others, you will never feel burdened. This does not mean that you have to be smiling all the time. The true smile is within. You can smile within when you understand that things are not so solid, not so real. Whatever you conceive of has no self-existing power — only the strength of compassion does. The force of this compassion is unobstructed. Give birth to the compassionate energy that dwells within your heart.

This compassionate quality can be perfected, just as fruit can one day ripen and produce sweet nectar. Try to see this potential in each individual, even when it has not been fully actualized. Then you will always respect and never denigrate others. With purification, the veils that obscure this inner luster will slowly fade away. Heartfelt concern for the world will radiate like soothing moonlight from the core of your heart.

Healing Self and Others

When we cannot enjoy unconditional freedom, we search for something outside ourselves and become the unwitting victims of destructive emotions. We seek to satisfy our hopes and desires, but even when we feel that we have reached that "promised land," there is never any lasting fulfillment. We continue to feel dissatisfied and yearn for more.

How do we begin to heal ourselves? True healing occurs when we begin to recover from the pain and disappointment we have suffered in our struggle to achieve happiness and success. Health is restored when we rest in the mind's natural state and we experience a sense of wholeness, free from conditional limitations. In the open space of our unconditional nature, we are content with ourselves, and we are able to communicate with others in a friendly and respectful way.

Happiness that is based on conditional circumstances is by nature impermanent and subject to change. When we have worldly success and gather friends and family around us, are these conditions dependable or stable? Can we rely on conditional pleasures for lasting fulfillment? We enjoy friends, food, and entertainment, but they seem just to sap our vigor. Can we stop in our tracks and look deeply within our being? We may find a more beautiful way to live and a healthier way to share our lives together.

Do you think it is possible to be free and not depend on external conditions for happiness? I feel that this is certainly possible because our true essence is free and unconditional. From this unconditional ground of being, everything arises as an expression of our true self. But when we do not recognize this radiance, we are lost in darkness. When we discover this luminosity, darkness will disappear instantaneously. Then we will know true inner wealth and true independence.

Our spiritual health depends on our capacity to embrace each moment. To be healed, we must see that there is nothing more precious than this moment — whether this moment looks promising or menacing. When we perceive the richness in this moment and are acutely aware that there may not be a next moment, we will passionately engage with our world. For much of our lives, we are so consumed by our internal dramas that we miss the enchantment and the magic. Cleansed of all negativity, we will discover a world that is perfect as it is.

Our mind creates our world. It is the mind that needs to be purified because everything is a reflection of mind. A clouded mirror will not reflect a brilliant world. It is up to us to decide how we want to perceive this world; it is our own doing and our own responsibility.

For the most part, the human mind depends on and clings to conditional circumstances that are changing every moment, every nanosecond. This causes us constant anxiety and distress. Understanding our shared predicament gives rise to sensitivity and caring for all beings. Then we can accept and embrace others just as they are. The less energy we expend trying to control what is uncertain and changing, the more we will be healed, moment by moment.

THE BODHISATTVA'S WAY

The bodhisattva is the ultimate expression of the compassionate heart. *Bodhisattva* is a Sanskrit word. The Tibetan term for bodhisattva is *chang chub sempa*. *Chang* means "fully trained" or "intuitive." *Chub* means "champion" or "expert," and *sempa* means "one with a courageous heart." The Tibetan term for bodhisattva connotes someone who is courageous, fully trained, and excels intuitively. So what has the bodhisattva mastered? What is this intuitive understanding of a bodhisattva? It is the expression of natural wisdom and compassion and the manifestation of the awakened state.

The way of the bodhisattva is very profound. It is true to say that a bodhisattva is kind and caring and acts in a selfless way. However, the meaning goes deeper than this. Bodhisattvas naturally and intuitively express their noble qualities. They do not seek recognition for good deeds, and they do not expect anything in return. Like the brilliant sun, they shine on everyone equally, without deliberate intention.

Bodhisattvas work tirelessly. Manifesting the boundless energy of the awakened state, they tackle every situation. They are willing to work on their own faults and weaknesses. They readily engage with others and do not shy away from any challenge. Bodhisattvas vow to be open to everyone, no matter what the circumstances, and they regard the thoughts and emotions of all beings as legitimate. The bodhisattva is willing to accept everyone just as they are, without prejudice or judgment. They never attempt to fool or deceive others. Every moment is rich with possibilities and is considered a perfect opportunity.

You can transform yourself into a true bodhisattva for your spouse, your children, your neighbors, and your friends. You should be resourceful because there are so many needs to be met and so many various ways that beings need help. It is truly beautiful to be so flexible and responsive. Be willing to connect to the very essence of every being — without judging them for their behavior or appearance. To truly touch the inner core of another's being is the practice of the bodhisattva.

When bodhisattvas drink a glass of water, they drink for the sake of all beings. As they free themselves of thirst, their wish is to quench the thirst of all beings. When bodhisattvas wear a new piece of clothing, they are joyful; they dress in good taste for the pleasure of all beings. The bodhisattva does not commit a single harmful or selfish act; everything is done with concern for others.

When you aspire to be a bodhisattva, you vow not to hurt anyone, not even your enemies. You vow to serve everyone, including your enemies. This is the best way to mature spiritually, no matter what your background or religious affiliation. When you take this vow, you embrace your true essence. There is one thing of which I am certain: *nothing will make you happier than benefiting other beings, and nothing will harm you more than hurting others*. Vowing to live your life in a meaningful way, you will never give up on humanity. One should feel comfortable being a bodhisattva. There is nothing more beautiful than seeing the whole world clearly and compassionately, with an open heart.

CHAPTER THIRTEEN

The Essence of Mind

THE HIDDEN JEWEL

The Buddha once noted, "When you help others, you serve me; when you hurt others, you sadden me." With keen insight, the Buddha understood the causes of suffering and how greatly we suffer due to our conflicting emotions and the forces of karma. Therefore, he taught his disciples to have compassion for all beings, as we are all subject to the hardships and afflictions of the human condition.

Buddhism places great emphasis on the truth of suffering and its causes. However, the Buddha also taught us that, if we follow the right path, suffering has an end. If all we see is suffering, we are seeing only half the picture. Understand that our innate nature is timelessly pure and unconditioned, free from the causes that create so much misery. Until we awaken, we will experience suffering. This truth can sensitize us to the torment that we all experience. With this heightened awareness, we will be less inclined to harm others. As we follow a path that progressively purifies the obscurations that veil our innate nature, our compassion for others will grow.

There was a poor man who suffered greatly, begging for scraps of food in the streets and wearing rags for clothing. One day, a stranger appeared and told the poor man that there was an enormous jewel buried in the ground under his shack. He explained to the beggar that he was actually the son of wealthy parents who had hidden this gem deep in the earth. The beggar was astonished by the stranger's tale, but he was not convinced it was true. However, the stranger finally persuaded the beggar to dig in the earth under his shack, where a magnificent and precious diamond was revealed.

The causes of suffering have no ground within the pure essence of mind. This pure essence is our very own treasure. When we discover this jewel that has always been ours, we will no longer feel deprived. When we develop conviction in our true nature, and follow a worthy path that purifies our obscurations, we can claim our inheritance and live in the richest and most meaningful way. Then, with care for all suffering beings, we can help them unearth their own priceless jewel.

Ocean of Wisdom

We live with the illusion of "self" and "other," yet both are creations of the conceptual mind. The mind reinforces the illusion of self and other with words and concepts and the continuity of habit.

One day, your friend becomes terminally ill, and you are distressed and think, "Oh, my dear friend is dying!" But when you fostered the notion of an everlasting friend, you ignored the reality of impermanence. You planted the seed for the pain and suffering of inevitable separation. Can you love your friend in every moment without getting stuck on your concept of friend? As you relate to your friend and carefully watch your thoughts coming and going, you will discover how the mind works. Is the nature of mind something tangible? Are thoughts truly existent?

All of our perceptions, thoughts, and feelings are like bubbles surfacing from the depths of a vast ocean. They arise from causes and conditions. They are dependent on the air and the motion of the water. All phenomena, including your thoughts and emotions, are dynamic expressions of energy, emerging and receding. You cannot grasp a bubble and hold it in your hand. Your family, friends, and possessions are like bubbles arising as the display of the mind's empty essence — the ocean of wisdom. The bubbles are not the source of your happiness — the ocean of wisdom is. Therefore, when the bubbles burst, your joy will not disappear. This effervescence is actually a wondrous display. With this understanding, you will be inspired to swim like a fish in the ocean of wisdom.

We do not have to view the continual cycle of birth and death as something negative; rather, we can find strength in it. Those who are afraid of birth and death attempt to accept or reject their experience, the bubbles on the ocean's surface. If you are clear about the nature of the bubbles, you can fearlessly dive right into this vast ocean and enjoy complete freedom. If a terrifying bubble pops up, you will not be tricked by its apparent existence. Let the bubble be, and it will burst by itself. Metaphorically speaking, as the bubbles burst, one after the other, they are naturally liberated with mindfulness. When you realize their essence, you are completely free from confusing projections.

The Nature of Thought

Constantly watch, constantly see how your mind is working and how your thoughts are coming and going. Always, you should try to apply this alertness in your daily life, to grasp the essence of the teachings of the Buddha. There is no end to your thoughts. Pay attention! Do not play with your thoughts. Do not be afraid of your thoughts. Do not run away from them. Do not cling to them. Do not ignore them. Do not look down on them. Do not identify with them.

Rather, see the nature of these thoughts. Where do these thoughts come from? Do thoughts truly exist in and of themselves? Do they have any power? What is the nature of thought? Figure this out. If you do not attach to your thoughts, they will have no power over you. Thoughts have no ground on which to exist. They are without substance, like the wind whistling through the trees. You should not engage with them or hang on to them. Just understand that all thoughts arise as energy, and this energy is the display of the mind's clear nature.

Recognize this state. However, do not become attached to this understanding, thinking that you have figured it all out; this kind of thinking is just hubris. When you actualize the natural state, the boastful "I" will dissipate like mist.

We are conditioned by our thoughts and feelings and get caught in their web. We think, "I have to achieve something for myself. I must work for my own happiness." It is all *me, me, me,* and *mine, mine, mine.* This is the cause of our suffering. Ask yourself, "Who am I, and what is mine?" If you can pay close attention to all of your thoughts and do not get caught in their web, you can live your life fully. Think about that freedom — every moment, not entangled or bound by "me" or "mine." Every moment will be an authentic moment and will manifest its pure potential. Imagine the possibilities! Think about that spontaneous energy!

LIKE A RIVER

Let's look clearly at the mind. Thoughts continuously appear. They arise without any hindrance. Ultimately, the energy of each thought is fresh, naked, and direct. Thoughts spontaneously appear and move in the mind naturally and innocently, like clouds passing through the sky. But it seems we have an irrepressible urge to manipulate our mental landscape. We accept and reject thoughts. We cling to pleasant thoughts and try to suppress disturbing thoughts. We are like unskillful artists tampering with a masterpiece by adding unnecessary strokes of paint.

There are spiritual teachers who recommend that we let go of our thoughts, or watch our thoughts, or stop our thoughts. Yet it is important to investigate and to question, Who is letting go of thoughts? Who is watching? Who is stopping?

A river is in constant motion, flowing and transforming. We picture it the same every day, but it is never the same. Every instant it is reconfigured; it is fresh and up to date. We apply the static label of "river," but there is no absolute, truly existing river, as we conceive of it.

The river just keeps flowing. In this fluidity there is constant change, but the river does not discriminate. The river does not cling to a beautiful flower floating on the surface. When the river carries a corpse, it is not repulsed. The river is not selective. It does not make judgments.

The energy of our true nature is like this river. Beautiful

sights do not enhance our true nature, and repulsive sights do not blemish it. Watching from the shore, we covet the lovely flowers and are revolted by the corpse. The watcher on the shore is ego, with a host of random preferences and predispositions. Not recognizing our wakeful nature, we are restless and confused. We cannot loosen and unwind. It is like an eager surfer waiting for his next wave. If a big wave comes, he is exhilarated, but after riding it out, he is waiting impatiently for the next one. The restlessness comes from the surfer's mind, not from the waves.

Thoughts and feelings are expressions of the mind. The open and spacious state of the mind is free from expectations, so it knows no disappointment. Ego is burdened with hopes and fears, and the obsessive need to control its parameters. This is the source of our suffering.

The Primordial Mirror

In the mirror of mind, everything reflects. What do you see in this mirror? You see wonderful things and terrible things, happy things and sad things, beautiful things and ugly things. I suggest seeing all these things as pure reflections — not as good or bad, not as beautiful or ugly. Like stars reflecting in a placid lake, nothing is out of place. Just look in this mirror and see these reflections clearly. Open your eyes. Just appreciate everything that appears in the mirror.

This mirror has the quality of your true nature, your fundamental goodness. It is basic sanity. It is timeless wisdom. Just appreciate this mirror and see the many things that reflect, coming and going. See the totality of it. The mirror's potential is limitless; it can reflect anything. Do not appreciate only the good things — appreciate everything, without passing judgment.

When images reflect within our mirror-like essence, we are in a rush to judge. We want to evaluate the reflection. Not recognizing the purity of this mirror-like essence, we appraise whatever appears in it. We identify with the reflection. How uncompassionate! How illegitimate to judge in this way, and how unfortunate to lose our freedom!

No matter what reflects within this essence, we can remain in a state of equanimity, without accepting or rejecting. Yet how often we pick and choose. This is a waste of energy, since the essence itself is completely free from acceptance and rejection.

So we are robbed of our natural freedom. It is senseless to grasp the beautiful reflection or reject the ugly one. How amazing it is to be totally free and unconditioned, without judgment, like the mirror!

Please see this clearly. See it directly. See it nakedly. Within the essence of mind, everything occurs, everything fades. This essence is pure, but how often do we experience this purity? How often do we recognize the essential nature of our being? Recognize that the nature of this mirror is unchanging. It has no beginning or end. Who would not appreciate this mirror? Isn't it interesting? It never rejects your ugly, angry face. It is so flexible and so genuine. So just sit for a while and be one with the mirror, where there is no perceiver separate from what is perceived.

The mirror's nature is fearless; ego is fearful. The mirror challenges and ego escapes. The mirror is dignified; ego is arrogant. The mirror does not cling to its reflections. Ego clings, thinking the reflections are real. The mirror is free from agitation and completely flawless. Ego is obscured and bound by constraints. Delusions arise when we cannot abide in this mirror-like essence, when we run away and try to become something other than what we are.

We should be intrigued by whatever manifests in the mirror. This mirror is flexible, but it does not waver. No amount of words can praise its wonderful qualities. It is something inexpressible, beyond description. Day and night, this mirror is capable of reflecting everything. It radiates peacefully, twenty-four hours a day.

Can you say that your judgment is correct when this mirror-like essence does not have any judgment whatsoever? Who judges your strength and your weakness? How amazing it is to be free from the fear of someone judging you or grading you! Only when you are completely one with your essence is the achievement of freedom possible.

Why are we so busy, rushing and running in circles, when we cannot accomplish anything by rushing or running? We will know complete satisfaction and contentment only when we are one with what is totally accomplished. To recognize and rest in the mind's pure nature is the ultimate accomplishment. How freeing it is to know that this complete perfection is within our reach. It has been with us forever. It is so close, yet we have ignored it. Isn't it time to realize this true essence?

CHAPTER FOURTEEN

Guidance of the Teacher

Blessings of the Lineage

My introduction to Buddhism came when I was just four years old. I remember playing with Buddhist ritual objects instead of the usual children's toys. It was at this time that I began to study and train in the Vajrayana Buddhist tradition. Later I attended a Tibetan Buddhist university near Deer Park, in Sarnath, where the Buddha gave his first sermon. After university, I met my root teacher — the one who introduced me to my true self-nature. I see my teacher as the Buddha himself. There is no difference between my teacher's wisdom and that of the Buddha. However, my teacher is kinder to me than the Buddha. Blessed by our auspicious connection in this life, he instructed me personally in the profound teachings, clarified my doubts, and introduced me to the unconditional enlightened essence.

I do not think that I have any great wisdom or realization to share; however, I feel very joyous and confident. I carry the nectar-like blessing of my enlightened teacher, who in turn carries the blessing of his master, from a lineage that can be traced back to the Buddha himself. These blessings are fresh and alive. You can rejoice and you can smile, since you possess the buddha nature within, the potential for awakening. The tremendous power of compassion is within your reach. Feel this possibility within you. All the masters of our lineage have achieved this enlightened quality and have lived their lives imbued with affection and caring for all beings.

THE NEED FOR A TEACHER

O ur innate nature is beyond all causal conditions, serene and completely calm. But if we do not actualize our innate nature, there will always be agitation and distress. Earnestly practicing meditation can help to free us from anxiety and stress. With the blessings of the teacher, the practice of meditation reveals the immovable ground where we can rest and remain at ease. There are many ways to practice meditation; one size does not fit all. You should find a teacher who can provide you with individual instruction that suits your temperament and lifestyle.

Since the Buddha taught us that we all possess innate wisdom, we may feel that the guidance of a teacher is not necessary and that we can tread the spiritual path unassisted. However, the ego can be quite tricky, like a con artist skilled in the art of deception. If we proceed without a teacher, we may lose precious time, and we may never realize our essence. On the path to awakening, there are myriad ways to get sidetracked. A do-it-yourself approach could be as messy as practicing brain surgery from a textbook.

It is very important to find a genuine teacher, a friend who can guide you and help you stand on your own two feet. A genuine teacher is one who has been trained by years of personal sacrifice, learning, and discipline. Such a teacher has subjugated his or her ego and manifests humility. Having received counsel and instructions from realized masters, he or she holds the power and blessings of a pure lineage. Genuine masters embody universal compassion and relate to each individual according to his or her needs. These great masters are rich in wisdom and will be trustworthy mentors and unfailing guides.

If you are fortunate to find a genuine teacher, approach him or her in a friendly and respectful manner. Your sincere interest in the teachings and your commitment to practice will elicit the teacher's guidance and support. You then find common ground where you can meet and establish rapport. This common ground is compassion, the warmth of kindness that aspires to alleviate the suffering of all. Meeting my own teacher in this profound way empowered me to tame my ego and give birth to a compassionate heart. Maintaining this perspective in your relationship with the teacher is essential.

When you feel rapport with the teacher, confusion subsides and compassion is spontaneously born in your heart the instant you think of him or her. Then you can be certain you have found your teacher. With the care and guidance of a capable teacher, you can build a solid foundation for spiritual growth. You will gain genuine strength and cultivate an authentic way of living.

Respect and Appreciation

In this tradition, remembering the kindness of the teacher and invoking his or her blessing can bring great joy and benefit. On the Buddhist path, we consider anyone who has granted us even one line of teaching to be worthy of our highest esteem. Respect and appreciation make us open and receptive vessels. When clay is warm and supple, the potter can mold it into beautiful shapes.

A humble person is flexible and can learn quickly. Pride and arrogance close the door on wisdom. Undermining self-conceit is a fundamental practice on the Buddhist path. Egotistic pride arises from ignorance, not wisdom. When wisdom illuminates, pride has no place.

Paying homage to the teacher draws forth the blessings of thousands of years of profound realization and wisdom. Our teacher holds the treasure of the Buddha's wisdom and is the embodiment of enlightenment. The kindness of my own teacher is beyond all measure. In his relationship with me, there is never a single moment of selfish thinking, only the radiance and warmth of his selfless care. Whether your teacher is near or far, you are always accompanied by the splendor of his or her natural wisdom and enormous richness. Within this sacred mandala,[1]

---

1. *Mandala* is a Sanskrit word that can literally be translated as "center and circumference." In this context, mandala is the realm of activity of the spiritual teacher and his students.

there is no cause for narrow-minded thinking and no place for half-hearted endeavor. We all possess the potential for awakening, yet it is best to have the guidance of a teacher who holds the power of his or her lineage and has a pure and direct link to the Buddha's blessings.

Unconditional Kindness
of the Master

Without a teacher, there is little possibility of complete awakening, unless one is unusually gifted with natural intelligence that can liberate one on the spot. Ordinary people like us need to follow a teacher. If we are attentive and take the teachings to heart, we will have the means to uncover our true nature.

In the capitalist world, with all of our freedoms and resources, we tend to think that we can easily access whatever we desire. But these profound and sacred teachings cannot be bought for any price. You have to approach these teachings from the proper perspective, understanding that you are suffering from the symptoms of karma and afflictive emotions. Think of yourself as a patient who is suffering from illness. You view the teacher as a skillful physician, and the teachings as healing medication. If you have trust in the physician, you will follow his or her prescription. If you practice the teachings of the Buddha sincerely, you will heal yourself from the chronic illness of samsara.

Only the teacher is unconditionally helpful and kind, showing us the most meaningful and honest way to live. Our parents and friends can be supportive, but their guidance is often ineffectual and does not address the root of our problems. They offer love, but their love is often conditional. The teacher is kind because he honors and respects our innate nature, and his kindness is unconditional. When experiencing the teacher's unconditional kindness, you will be inspired to manifest devotion to the teacher and so honor your true self.

Having devotion and respect for the teacher will empower you to live in the moment. Living fully in the moment is the greatest gift that you can give to yourself and the best offering you can give to your teacher. The manifestation of the teacher is the expression of your essence. With faith and trust in your teacher, you will realize the essence of your being. Fervent prayer and devotion can swiftly unveil your innate nature. You will never stray from this essence when you have genuine devotion. As a great Buddhist master once said, "When the words of the teacher enter your heart, it is like holding a jewel in the palm of your hand."

From the time of the Buddha, the state of awakening has been realized by all of the great lineage masters. The teacher represents the awakened state and is a great inspiration for others. Union with the teacher occurs when you recognize the teacher's wisdom-mind within the core of your being and become one with your true self-nature. At this time the teacher's realization is inseparable from you. True devotion is deep love, loyalty, and dedication; it is not mindless or foolish fanaticism. Devotion to the teacher is the most revered and profound practice of our lineage. With sincere devotion for the teacher, you will achieve true realization and genuine trust in your primordial essence.

The aim of practice is to remain at ease by becoming familiar with your true nature. Remaining at ease is the key. The teacher is interested in sharing this truth, which is his way of serving his own teacher. The teacher can show you the way, but first you must be deserving of his guidance. Your attainment comes from your devotion to the teacher and diligence in your practice.

The teacher is an indispensable guide on the path of discovery. The joy and satisfaction you ultimately experience is the blessing of your teacher. Recollecting this, devotion and respect for the teacher come effortlessly. Your love and concern for all beings flow naturally. You are one with your teacher's wisdom-mind and his compassionate heart. With these signs, you know you are on the right path. Without them, you are missing the heart and the essence.

THE TEACHER IS EVERYWHERE

When you respect the teacher, you acknowledge your own noble qualities. The teacher is the expression of your own goodness. When you invoke the teacher, you are summoning the goodness that exists within you. By paying respect to the teacher, you can master all situations. When you connect to the teacher and his or her lineage, you will be capable of maintaining your integrity twenty-four hours a day.

You will find the teacher everywhere. A sparrow singing in the garden is the melody of your teacher's counsel. A lush, green forest is the form of your teacher, beckoning you to celebrate this wonderful life. The swift motion of a stream in the woods is the gesture of your teacher, demonstrating that your life is passing quickly and that you should seize the moment with vigilance and awareness. When the trees change to beautiful colors in autumn, the scattering of leaves in the wind is the teacher's discourse on impermanence.

With this sacred connection, you will always have guidance and spiritual inspiration, whether the teacher is near or far. You will never be tricked or seduced by alluring appearances, which inevitably become sources of attachment and pain. On the Buddhist path, you are extremely fortunate if you can forge this precious link with a genuine teacher and a pure lineage.

GESTURE OF DEVOTION

If you apply yourself to the practice of meditation, you will be able to supervise yourself. You will be responsible for your actions. When you can maintain clarity and wakefulness, you will attend to all that you encounter with intelligence and skill, and you will not need the physical form of the teacher always by your side. The teacher's wisdom will be inseparable from you.

When you show respect for the teacher, you honor your own innate wisdom. When you recognize your innate nature, you appreciate yourself. When you appreciate who you are, you will naturally devote time and energy to relate to your teacher. You are practicing for yourself, though not in a selfish way. You develop confidence in the indestructible quality that exists within you. When you have this confidence, you will respect yourself and you will respect the teacher.

The gesture you use to show respect for the teacher is known in Sanskrit as the *anjali mudra*. You bring the palms of your hands together at the level of your heart and pray to the teacher for his or her blessing. When you join your hands in this way, it is not an ordinary, empty gesture. It is performed sincerely, with a feeling of enormous gratitude and appreciation. With trust and conviction, you surrender to the natural wisdom embodied in your teacher.

You touch your heart center with your hands joined. The right hand symbolizes compassion and the left hand symbolizes

wisdom. Like bringing positive and negative poles together, join-
ing hands in this way brings luminosity. Light radiates from your
heart when you turn on the switch. Suddenly, there is no gloom
or darkness. Then you can smile and rejoice. Genuine devotion
brings true clarity straight into your heart.

Luminous Teacher

When it comes to spiritual practice, it can be difficult at times to persevere. No matter how weary or disillusioned we may become with the affairs of our everyday lives, we still take solace in the belief that there are better times ahead. There are so many enticing possibilities and alluring sidetracks, so many obstacles that can impede our spiritual practice or, worse, bring it to a standstill.

The fact of the matter is, there are very few who practice these teachings with genuine conviction. This is unfortunate because a rare and precious opportunity is being missed. There is a real possibility that we will play games, claiming that we are on a spiritual path by doing this and that practice, following such-and-such teacher. However, we have to be honest with ourselves. On our spiritual journey, if we have to take some bitter medicine, we must be willing to swallow it completely. Until we are able to purify our negative karma and obscurations, we will not uncover the profound nature of our unconditional essence.

No wonder that, after attaining realization, Shakyamuni Buddha was determined to stay in the forest and remain silent. After many fervent requests from seekers, he finally came forth to preach, but he never assumed that his teachings alone could liberate beings from their suffering. The Buddha made it clear that he could lead a horse to water, but he could not make it drink. Therefore, the lineage of the Lord Buddha is not a pretentious one.

Before we begin our journey, we have to understand what we are doing and why. We should not follow anyone blindly. We must use our intelligence. We should examine and question until we have secured some confidence and trust. Then, and only then, can we progress further.

If you follow this path sincerely, at times you may feel that you are very much alone. It may be hard to fit in because the shapes and colors that surround you do not seem natural. You may not care to associate yourself with these disturbing shapes and colors. But do not be discouraged. You should feel lucky that you are following an unfailing path that leads to a truly worthy destination.

If you are a genuine practitioner, you do not go searching for a babysitter whenever you are having a bad time. You do not look for a shoulder to cry on. Whatever happens, you face the situation and handle it fully. When there is deep pain and sorrow, you must be willing to confront it, right on the spot. Face every moment as if there were no next moment. Do not take superficial comfort in the past, or place blind trust in the future. With clear awareness, you tackle the moment just as it is.

When you establish a connection with a qualified teacher and persevere in your practice, you will benefit from your devotion. However, the moment you are distracted and lose awareness, in the blink of an eye, you will sever your connection to the teacher. When you are alert and undistracted, your relationship with the teacher will be pure and profound. Then you will be one with the teacher's wisdom and compassion. This is the luminous teacher, and there is nothing more profound than this. The teacher who introduces you to your true nature is the luminous teacher in physical form. You value his or her immense kindness, and respond by taking the teachings and instructions to heart.

You miss the teacher the moment you become distracted. Thus, do not allow your mind to wander. You miss the teacher when you grow attached to the teacher. Therefore, do not cling to the teacher. In the luminous teacher there is complete clarity, and this relationship is enduring. In this tradition, while you are walking, you visualize the teacher above your head or on your right shoulder. When having a cup of tea, you mentally offer the first sip to the teacher with gratitude, and when eating a meal, you offer your food to the teacher with mindfulness. As you fall asleep, the teacher dwells in the center of your heart, and you sleep peacefully throughout the night.

When you are not distracted, what is there to meditate on? You need to meditate only when there is mental wandering. Preserving the continuity of awareness is the ultimate meditation. To be able to rest in this pure awareness is the supreme blessing of the teacher. You wish to be inseparable from this realization and hold it close to your heart. You feel as if you want to be with the teacher day and night. No other relationship can compare to this. When you unite with the wisdom mind of the teacher, unconditional luminosity — the true face of your being — is revealed.

CHAPTER FIFTEEN

Fearlessness

LOOKING FOR HEAVEN

We often try to alter and control the circumstances of our lives, and this makes it difficult to discover an authentic way of being. We want to improve things because we are blind to the beauty of the world as it is.

The spiritual path is not a way to insulate ourselves from adversity. As we begin to practice meditation, we might feel as if we were taking a bitter medication with unpleasant side effects. As we slow down our discursive minds, we can experience much heartache and pain. Actually, the pain has always been there, buried under the surface. We have simply been covering it up with so much physical, mental, and emotional activity, like an addict masking suffering with a narcotic.

When pure energy is distorted by our confusion and self-grasping, it manifests in harmful and destructive ways. We feel threatened by distressing thoughts and emotions and attempt to escape in a fog of frenetic activity. The more we try to escape, the more ensnared we become. So we fantasize and envision a different way of life that has little to do with reality. However, instead of liberating ourselves from pain and anxiety, we strengthen the ego and never have the opportunity to find freedom. We are not fully present in our moment-to-moment experience, so we cannot embody an authentic way of being.

From the beginning, we should ask ourselves why we are following a spiritual path. It seems that we often pursue spirituality with the desire to reach "heaven." No matter how much we struggle, we are determined to find beauty and peace in our lives that are stable and everlasting. But we are shaken when faced with perturbing and unpleasant situations. Suspecting that we cannot sustain the serenity and security that we have envisioned, we become fearful and insecure. We begin to panic. Unless we change our fundamental approach to spirituality, no matter where we turn, we will never find a path to lasting fulfillment.

Each moment of our lives presents a new challenge. We have to be poised and ready. We have to be prepared to deal with unsettling events as they arise. This is why we practice. This, in essence, is the ultimate meditation practice: learning to handle every challenge.

How should we relate to every challenge? In the *Heart Sutra*, the Buddha's teachings on wisdom, it says, "Since there is no obscuration of mind, there is no fear." When we can fully embrace things as they are, we can relate to every moment without fear. Natural fearlessness exists within every being and within the nature of all things. Our fundamental nature has no fear. We will understand that fear is not an insurmountable obstacle when we realize that the beauty and order that we cling to — and fear to lose — are without essence. Everything is conditional and subject to change. The belief that we need to manipulate and control things is unfounded. This mistaken way of thinking is the obscuration we need to purify.

In the Face of Uncertainty

A s the saying goes, "Familiarity breeds contempt." However, the ego thrives on routine and clings to what is familiar. In the face of uncertainty, ego is as skittish as a spooked horse. To move beyond fear, be aware of fear as it arises. Watch closely when the slightest stirrings of unease and apprehension begin to provoke alarm. Practicing this way, you will begin to confront your worst fears.

When you are one with the fear itself, you will experience luminous clarity. Facing fear with awareness, you will experience its shifting and intangible nature. You cannot quite pin it down. Fear can feel like an insurmountable barrier, but within this clarity, fear has no dwelling place. You might be meeting with your boss in the morning. On your way to work, you begin to ruminate about what you will say and how your boss will react. You begin to feel apprehensive. Recognizing these thoughts as baseless projections frees you from their grip and brings you back to clarity in the present moment.

Until you are one with this clarity, you will not be free from fear. However, this penetrating clarity can reveal a deeper level of fear, as you find yourself in uncharted terrain. The unconditional state of being is well beyond the domain of egocentric mind. We have no clue how to function in this vast and unstructured space. There is no role for the ego to play, and this can be very frightening. For some semblance of safety and security, we rely on ego's reference points and cling to our concepts. With the practice of meditation, we can grow familiar with the groundless quality of fear itself.

We can empathize with others because we all experience fear. You cannot say to others, "Do not be afraid; it will be all right." This is an approach that is both intellectually simplistic as well as crude and heavy-handed. When you say, "There's no need to be afraid," you imply you have no fear yourself. However, in truth, you are fearful as well. That is the reason you say such things. When you remain in the clarity of the fearless state, you can truly help to free others from fear. This is the way of the enlightened ones.

Look Inside the Fear

When faced with fear, we may be timid or we may be aggressive, but there is neutral ground where we do not have to act like wimps or bullies. Beyond the hesitation and defensiveness of ego, there is awareness and clarity. The essence of fear is fearlessness. This state is naturally heroic and does not require any reinforcement. How fortunate it is if we can recognize this natural state of fearlessness.

How does fear arise? Where does it come from? Where does it go? If you look inside the fear with the clarity of awareness, you will not need to resort to evasive tactics or aggressive maneuvers. However, for the most part, we are ill-prepared to handle fear. When faced with danger, if we are not fully present and awake, fear will overwhelm us. On the outside, we may look self-assured in an expensive suit or silk dress, but fear lurks within because there is very little awareness.

We may assume that a financial crisis or broken relationship is the cause of our fear and insecurity. In truth, we are fearful when we do not recognize the indestructible quality of our true essence. This essence is unborn and undying, and it is naturally fearless.

Every occurrence in our life, every thought and feeling, is simply the dynamic display of this essence. The experience of fear is also a display of this essence. But we attempt to cover up our fears and hide them under the carpet. We act with bravado, or we become aggressive. We imagine ourselves to be great soldiers, bankers, lawyers, or politicians. We can be terribly hard on ourselves. Time passes and we slowly lose our physical strength and mental acuity as we get closer to death. We waste our time and dissipate our energy pretending to be something we are not. We labor hard at boosting our image and enhancing our reputation, without ever discovering the inner beauty that is our true essence.

Fearlessness and the View

We have to recognize the nature of fear before we can experience fearlessness. We cannot simply run away from fear. We have to get close to it. We have to be intimate with it. Fear does not arise without cause. If we understand the nature of fear, we can move beyond it. We have to be patient and give everything some space.

Everyone has personal views. However, when you become attached to your view, you become very rigid, like plywood that will not bend. This disturbs your sense of equilibrium, and you lose your sense of humor. You no longer have control of your view; rather, your view has control of you. It would be analogous to a man loving his girlfriend so obsessively that she feels compelled to run away from him. He becomes far too close due to his loneliness, insecurity, and fear.

The Buddha taught us that the highest view is to be free from all views. This supreme view will not remain with those who are insecure or fearful. This view will not stay with those who are territorial. This view is confident and complete in its own place. There is nothing that is outside the perimeter of this view. Those who understand this all-encompassing view are always fearless. Due to the fact that this view is complete in its own place, it does not need any manipulation. This is the profound view.

This view is very naked and direct. Because it is so naked, like a live electric wire without insulation, you have to be cautious.

You know what will happen if you touch it carelessly. If you are skillful and know how to handle the wire, you can harness its power and enjoy an abundance of light. In our tradition, it is taught that raw thoughts and emotions must be handled with awareness and skill. Otherwise, there is a real danger that we will hurt ourselves and others through careless and coarse indulgence.

Many of us are afraid to get close to this wire. We try to escape, rather than learning how to work with its power. There is an abundant supply of electricity, but not so many electricians. There may be many who are intrigued by this view, but only a fortunate few who learn how to benefit from it. If you are not interested in learning how to harness this power, do not be too hard on yourself. It's okay. One can take a more gradual approach. There is a time and place for everything.

Everything we perceive, think, and feel emanates from this wide-open view. This is the fearless view. This view is absolutely unbiased. It is completely free from discrimination. We tend to think that we are better than others. We fabricate a hierarchy in our minds and place ourselves on the highest tier. This sort of bias does not exist at the beginning; it comes afterward. In timeless purity, there is no corruption and no judgment.

Light and warmth radiate from the sun. As the sun shines on the earth, it does so without discrimination, equally illuminating all. But if we lack the proper view, we might blame the sun for not being bright enough or warm enough. Perhaps the sun is too low in the sky or there are too many dark clouds. But the sun is always radiating, whether we can see its light or not. This is the absolute view. This eternally brilliant light exists within every individual. The wisdom that exists within you is the best teacher.

This self-arising awareness is your ultimate friend and your dearest companion.

This wisdom is always pure, and this purity brings freedom. There is fearlessness in this basic purity. It is like a lotus flower. Although it is planted in the mud, the flower is always free of stain. It draws nourishment from the mud but is never tainted by the mud. When it blossoms, it is spotless and radiant. It is completely free from the mire that surrounds it. You do not have to reject what you have or start over. Just remain in the mud and grow. Draw on its moisture and nutrients for energy.

Within this purity, everything is accomplished and complete. We can develop unwavering confidence in this view. Wherever there is mind, there is the potential for actualizing this unblemished view. We can share our warmth and kindness with everyone — there is more than enough space in this primordial purity. This view is not narrow or limited in any way; it is vast and expansive. So we can explore, and we can look far beyond our limited views. Then we have the ultimate view, and there will be fearlessness in every moment of our lives.

CHAPTER SIXTEEN

Abundant Wealth

Like a Small Flower

We can face this world that is full of desire, anger, and pride — full of tumultuous emotions — with confidence in our unconditional nature. We do not have to adopt the guise of a powerful warrior; we can appear in the form of a small flower — gentle, subtle, graceful, and unassuming. Although lotus flowers grow in mud, they blossom in flawless purity. We are rooted in the mire of negative emotions, but our true nature is imbued with goodness. Therefore, we can take our stand mindfully, with a firm and unwavering sense of confidence.

All human beings are subject to myriad forms of suffering. We can help to pacify the negativity of others, not with aggression, but with peaceful determination and self-assurance. In the absolute sense, everyone is equal; every being is as worthy as the Buddha. The Buddha taught us that all beings deserve our kindness and respect. Recognize the basic goodness that is innate in all beings.

When you speak, make it meaningful. If what you have to say is not helpful, it is best to remain silent. Frivolous speech just creates disharmony and discord. As the old saying goes, empty vessels make the most noise. The less you speak, the less opposition you will encounter. Refraining from constant chatter can indeed be a refreshing and sacred meditation. Bereft of a kind and caring heart, your speech is not likely to reach others, but sincere words graced with genuine kindness can touch the hardest of hearts.

On an Island of Gold

When you experience the lucidity of pure awareness, simply gazing at someone's face can be an enriching experience. If you are incapable of seeing clearly, it is as if you are
blind. In this context, blindness is not seeing and appreciating
the colorful and vibrant qualities of whatever you encounter in
your life.

If you can see your friend's face clearly, without a trace of
obscuration, you will appreciate her life in a pure and innocent
way. You will value her presence more deeply. You will not find
any flaws in your friend or see any reason for conflict. Conflict
merely indicates that you do not perceive the preciousness of life
itself. When you see the preciousness of human life, you will not
feel that your point of view is superior. You will be considerate
and understanding. Realizing the preciousness of human life can
lead one to the gateway of ultimate realization. It is such a great
joy to perceive this preciousness!

Have love and respect for yourself. If you fail to appreciate
the worthiness of your own life, you will not have concern for
others. You will find faults in others and lose sight of the preciousness of human life. There is no bigger failing than this.

If you find yourself on an island where everything is made
of gold, you should not go home empty-handed. Recognize and
embrace this treasure. Enjoy some of this gold and relish this
supremely valuable thing we call life. When you realize how

much you have wasted your time with mundane concerns, tears of sorrow will come. On the other hand, appreciating your good fortune will bring tears of joy. Tears of joy will come when you pray to the teacher within. When you look deep within yourself, you perceive the infallible nature of the teacher. You recognize the potential that exists in yourself and in every being. Then you will feel respect for the teacher and find wonder in every form you see, in every sound you hear, and in everything you touch.

Ceaseless Flow of Nectar

The compassion of the teacher is like a majestic mountain covered in dazzling white snow, and your devotion is like the bright sun. When the warmth of your devotion melts the snow on the mountain, a ceaseless flow of nectar will quench your thirst and end all deprivation. This sweet nectar is the blessing of the teacher.

The strength of our devotion for the teacher is not constant. Bright days turn gloomy and clouds conceal the brilliance of the sun. When your devotion to the teacher is strong and unwavering, nothing will stop you from enjoying complete freedom. Good and bad, positive and negative, and high and low will dissolve into space. White and black clouds will dissipate. The sun's rays will shine forth, nectar will stream from the snow-covered mountain, and you will taste the elixir that is your real life.

You will no longer thirst for the mundane or desire to taste what is ordinary. The blessings of the teacher will instill you with reverence. You will find great joy in simple things. The world may not change, but your perceptions will be more lively and fresh. You will not get lost in flights of fancy when you are busy enjoying your world in a direct and uncontrived way.

With resilience, you will move through your life with the skill and precision of an accomplished dancer. Every move a skillful dancer makes is part of a seamless and delightful performance. If you value your life, it will become like a beautiful dance. Everything you experience — all of your thoughts and feelings — will be your dancing partners, and you will move in synch with their rhythms. Here, you will find real exhilaration and joy. You will become a consummate dancer, and you will perform with poise and self-assurance.

IN THE PRESENCE OF THE MASTER

In our tradition, we consider every day to be an auspicious day. At any moment, in any circumstance, there is the possibility to actualize the true essence of our being, which we call buddhahood. Hence, every day and every moment is very precious. In a way, enlightenment is very near to us, so we should always trust in our potential for awakening. Otherwise, opportunities could easily elude us. In this tradition, we believe that we can attain liberation in this very lifetime by skillfully utilizing our precious human life, meeting a genuine teacher, following the path with conviction, and practicing diligently. What's more, "in this very lifetime" does not necessarily mean at some point far in the future. It could mean in this very moment!

Feel the urgency to practice well, as if there were no tomorrow. The practice is to smile sincerely, since you may not have another opportunity. The practice is to greet your friend warmly, since you may never see your friend again. The practice is to show respect for your teacher, since you do not know what tomorrow will bring. The practice is to give freely, since it may be your last chance to experience the joy of giving. Apply these teachings and practice them well!

If your friend is disagreeable with you, stop and reflect that there is no fault in you or in your friend. Disagreement happens because we are not seeing the whole picture. You should allow space for events to evolve and reveal themselves. Allow room for every thought. If you allow space between your first thought and second thought, between your first feeling and second feeling, you will have clarity and understanding.

When you allow breathing room for your thoughts and feelings, you will not be impulsive or rash in your reactions. Within this space you will generate respect and see beauty. Space punctuates your confusion and enhances your awareness. It is the basis for all meditation. All spiritual activity must be grounded in this understanding. Enlightenment itself is based on this understanding.

In our tradition, the great masters give you all the space you need. When you are in the master's presence, confusion vanishes and there is simple space to dwell in. No matter how disorderly things seem to be, no matter how sharp the contrast between black and white in your life, it all feels inconsequential when you are in the master's presence. Manifesting space, the master is not carried away by your first thought or second thought, and everything becomes magical. Even if the master has nothing to say, no words with which to console you, you leave feeling pacified and content because the master has just shared with you a glimpse of this infinite space.

UNDERSTANDING

In closing, I strongly urge you to practice. These teachings must be applied to your daily life — they must be put into practice — in order to have any effect and lead to true realization.

The practice is to be gentle. The practice is to be kind. The practice is to be understanding. Be understanding of your own behavior. Be understanding of your friend's behavior and of your foe's behavior. Be understanding of everyone's behavior and their way of thinking. If you can maintain this level of comprehensive understanding, you will require nothing more. Always aspire to be the most understanding person on this earth! Then you will relate to everything profoundly. There will be nothing further you need to accomplish. With this alone, you will have accomplished everything.

If you lack understanding, even if you sit straight in the lotus position like the perfect Buddha, you are not the Buddha. Without understanding, even if you are a learned Buddhist scholar, you are not a true Buddhist. With understanding, you are a Buddhist in so many ways. You do not need to have one shape, one color, or one form to be a Buddhist. In any way you are, you are a Buddhist, and you are a follower of the great enlightened ones.

You do not need to perform a single ritual of this tradition. You do not need to study a single Buddhist text. As long as you are kind, compassionate, and understanding, you are a true follower of the Buddha. This will prolong your life and allow you to live in comfort and ease. Ultimately, this will make you happy, and this will make others happy as well.

This medicine of great understanding will cure every disease. This is the most profound matter, so take it to heart. Remember, this is your life, so *do not waste it*. We are all getting closer and closer to death, so take responsibility to live your life fully. Seize the moment by living now. Make your life meaningful. At the moment of death, you do not want to be full of regrets, feeling you have wasted a precious opportunity. So live purposefully. Live kindly. Live with mindfulness.

When you practice in this way, the teacher is with you. When you are kind, compassionate, and understanding, the luminous teacher abides in the center of your heart. This is how one should see the teacher, and this is how one should practice these teachings. In this way, one will reap great rewards from this profound and sacred tradition of the Great Perfection.

May this benefit all beings.

AFTERWORD: QUESTIONS ABOUT LOVE, WORK, AND LIFE WITH SHYALPA RINPOCHE

QUESTION: *From your lifelong observation, why do people suffer?*

HIS EMINENCE SHYALPA TENZIN RINPOCHE: When we are born, we have obtained the beautiful and priceless gift of life. As we get older, we face sickness, old age, and death. Human beings cannot live forever, but we try to live as well and as happily as possible. However, human beings are controlled by the disturbing emotions of desire, greed, anger, jealousy, pride, ignorance, and discontentment. In general, lacking awareness of their true essence, people look for happiness in all the wrong places and suffer from their ignorance.

QUESTION: *Many people seem to work very hard, earn a lot of money, and still feel dissatisfied with their lives. How do we find a way to pursue a spiritual life while living in a material world?*

RINPOCHE: Why do we work? In the beginning, we work in order to feed ourselves, have shelter, and meet our basic needs. Over time, we become spoiled and take these things for granted. We gradually forget why we are working and expect much more from our jobs. We want to acquire status, wealth, and respect. Neglecting our spiritual development, we pursue material success and forget about our precious breath. We should value and enjoy our work, but our work should not totally consume us.

When we become attached and addicted to our jobs, we forget how precious our life is.

We come to this world for a purpose, and we need to discover the meaning of our existence. Isn't the purpose of life to find true freedom and discover your true self? Freedom does not mean sleeping until noon and not having to work; freedom is the ability to channel your creativity through your work. To live a spiritual life is to remain unattached and truly free, while functioning in the material world.

QUESTION: *What about people who are trying to lead a meaningful life but feel lost and depressed?*

RINPOCHE: We all need a teacher who can guide us and introduce us to the secret essence of life. You definitely cannot buy the teachings with money or influence. You have to be deserving of these sacred teachings. You need to have respect and devotion for a genuine teacher, who can successfully guide you on your spiritual path. The teacher can help you find your strength by showing you how to celebrate life. Having the care and guidance of a teacher will ensure that you do not get lost in confusion or suffer from endless depression.

QUESTION: *What advice do you give your students who struggle to live in the moment?*

RINPOCHE: In my tradition, we try to empower people and give them an understanding of their true nature and what their purpose is in life. Everyone, even the rich and powerful, has insecurities. I try to help my students gain freedom from insecurity and fear by introducing them to their unconditional intelligence, which is the most fulfilling and blissful state that one can experience. I feel people should focus on discovering who they are, and realize how precious this life is. We need to learn how beneficial it is to be compassionate. We should strive to reach enlightenment, so that we can free ourselves and free others from suffering. Discovering the absolute knowledge from which we are inseparable is the most essential thing. This knowledge has to be revealed through spiritual practice and the blessings of the teacher and his or her lineage.

QUESTION: *Many people feel very attached to their possessions. What advice do you have for people who are deeply entrenched in the material world?*

RINPOCHE: Life is a priceless gift to be celebrated. When people feel angry and upset, I ask them to imagine that they have only two or three breaths before death. Then, I ask them to think about what is most important to them. The most important thing is our breath, our life. Make the most out of your life and live as if there is no tomorrow. Be kind to your neighbors; you do not know if you will see them again. Share your wealth; you do not know if you will have another chance. Live as if this is your last moment. Try to celebrate with whomever you are with and take joy in whatever you are doing. Don't take things too seriously. Everything in life is truly ephemeral and dreamlike. If you have material wealth, it is good to give to charity. If you hoard your wealth, you will be spiritually poor and incapable of celebrating life.

QUESTION: *What is happiness to you? Helping others makes one happy, and partying makes one happy. What is the relationship between happiness and spirituality?*

RINPOCHE: For me, real happiness is complete freedom. The only thing that can cause me to lose my freedom is the workings of my habituated mind. So I have to learn how to relate to my mind skillfully. If we want to be happy, we should start by remembering that everyone wants to be happy. We have to be concerned about everyone's happiness, not just our own. There are over seven billion people on this earth, as well as countless other creatures. If you try to exist in your own small world of happiness, you cannot truly be happy. To pursue happiness only for yourself is very shortsighted. If you want to be happy, think about how to make others happy, and act on that.

QUESTION: *How can charity promote happiness?*

RINPOCHE: When you are generous, you find fulfillment in giving. Charity is a way of celebrating your life. I feel that people who are generous have a more rewarding experience than those on the receiving end. Generosity brings strength and freedom by lessening your attachment. When you are able to share your wealth, generosity becomes the means to accomplish your own goals. You should not become a slave to your wealth. To be charitable is to live life fully!

QUESTION: *What is "living in the moment"?*

RINPOCHE: Living in the moment is freedom from the past, present, and future. It is freedom from time, concepts, and conditions. It is freedom from any expectation of reward. Living in the moment is fully embracing this moment, and this moment is completely perfect as it is. Living in the moment is everything.

QUESTION: *Many young people are addicted to Facebook and Twitter, or spend their entire day on their iPhones and iPods. Do you think these technological developments prevent people from living in the moment?*

RINPOCHE: Many brilliant and ingenious people have created these products for our benefit. Such innovations can help humankind to progress and grow. But if we use technology for destructive purposes, such as nuclear weapons, we can destroy our lives. Tools such as the Internet or cell phones can enhance our lives if we use them with a positive motivation, for the benefit of ourselves and others. The point is not the tool itself, but how we use it.

That said, tools like Facebook and Twitter could trap us in meaningless distraction. We must remember that the most satisfying thing is to live fully. If we cannot be truly satisfied and content with ourselves, the next new gadget will soon leave us bored when the novelty wears off. Technology in itself is not the cause of our problems. We need to be aware of the confusing thoughts and emotions that bombard us while we use these tools. We need to learn how to handle these intruders! I recommend everybody spend at least five minutes each day without music, video games, cell phones, or the Internet. Be with yourself in a quiet place. Just meditate and relate to your mind with awareness.

QUESTION: *What do you think of women pursuing beauty in this world of glamour, fashion, and innovative cosmetic surgeries?*

RINPOCHE: Women are beautiful when they are natural and carefree. Cosmetic surgery, makeup, and fashion are tools that can enhance a woman's beauty, but they are not forever. The feminine qualities that a woman is born with are enduring. The ultimate beauty is to be oneself. A woman should know herself and be proud of her feminine qualities — there is nothing more attractive than that. Tara, the Buddhist deity, proclaimed, "Until all beings attain enlightenment, I will remain in the female form for their benefit." So please seek and find inner liberation, like the most beautiful goddess, Tara.

QUESTION: *What is your view on desire?*

RINPOCHE: We are born with desire. We should not resist what we are born with; rather, we should learn to utilize and channel our energy. Life is worth celebrating. Compassionate healers mix poison and herbs to make effective medicines. Desires can be channeled, released, and transformed; the key is how you deal with the energy of desire. The liberated energy of desire does not have harmful consequences.

QUESTION: *The Internet has made it easier to watch pornography or have a one-night stand, but it seems that people just have more desire and can never be satisfied. Why?*

RINPOCHE: Those who watch pornography or have one-night stands are seeking gratification from external sources. If you use sexuality only to satisfy your physical needs, you will never be fully satisfied. A sexual relationship of mind and body will provide complete satisfaction. A Tibetan Buddhist prayer states that the greatest feast is to satisfy your partner. Sex should not be about selfish desire; it is a feast for the celebration of life. My advice is to celebrate your own life and feel love toward everyone, including yourself. Admire yourself and be proud of yourself. Enjoy being with yourself and be content.

QUESTION: *How does one face oneself honestly while fulfilling one's social responsibilities?*

RINPOCHE: Honesty is to live genuinely in this moment without needing to fabricate anything. When you have something to hide, then you lose contact with the moment and you miss the moment's vitality and energy. Honestly facing oneself, and acknowledging one's weaknesses, is a good practice, as we all can overcome obstacles. Everyone has weaknesses. People will understand and forgive our weaknesses. When we face ourselves honestly, we will truly know what our purpose is and what our social responsibilities are.

QUESTION: *You have led a spiritual life for over forty years now. Have you ever felt like pursuing another career?*

RINPOCHE: No, not really. For me, spirituality is about having complete freedom to live in the moment. I don't think of teaching as my job. My responsibility is to live freely, to the fullest extent. No matter what I am doing — whether it is teaching, relating to friends, or answering questions — I feel like I am communicating with others by sharing our precious lives together. How often does one have a chance to talk with others about one's life? So it is most important that I spend my time compassionately, by caring about you and the fact that you are interested in listening to me. As far as I'm concerned, I am trying my best to connect with people, as well as enjoy my own achievement and realization. This is why I am comfortable traveling and assisting others as much as I can. This is how I practice and express my caring and concern for others. My career will always be to experience true freedom and to express my sincere compassion and love for all sentient beings.

Glossary

afflictions: (Skt. *klesha*) Attachment, aversion, pride, envy, and ignorance, which cause disturbance in the mind and obscure its pure nature.

all-accomplishing wisdom: One of the five wisdoms. The impure energy of envy is transformed into all-accomplishing wisdom, which spontaneously and effortlessly benefits oneself and others.

blessing: The Tibetan word for blessing means "transforming magnificent potential." This magnificent potential is the development of virtuous qualities and the lessening of unwholesome qualities. An accomplished teacher can confer blessings on a receptive student.

bodhisattva: (Skt.) With conviction in the innate buddha nature, a bodhisattva makes a firm resolution to work courageously for the awakening of all beings.

Buddha: (Skt.) A fully awakened being, free from all obscurations and replete with enlightened wisdom qualities.

buddha nature: The ultimate, awakened nature of mind. All sentient beings possess this nature and have the potential to become enlightened.

compassion: One of the four boundless qualities. The genuine wish that all beings become free from suffering and its causes.

dedication of merit: Offering the positive energy of one's practice for the benefit of all beings, including oneself.

devotion: Deep respect and appreciation for the enlightened qualities of the teacher, and trust in the teacher's capacity to help lead one to one's own enlightened nature.

Dharma: (Skt.) The truth as taught by the enlightened ones. It can also refer to phenomena, meaning objects or events.

discriminative wisdom: One of the five wisdoms. The impure energy of desire is transformed into discriminative wisdom, which clearly distinguishes the qualities of all phenomena without confusion.

dualistic fixation: The mind's grasping at relative concepts such as "self" and "other," believing them to truly and independently exist.

emptiness: (Skt. *shunyata*) The absence of anything that can be grasped at by the dualistic mind. The essence of mind does not possess any limiting characteristics, yet it reflects all phenomena.

enlightenment: Full awakening to the ultimate nature of mind and reality. It is the state beyond all obscurations, and the complete actualization of all positive qualities.

five wisdoms: The five aspects of enlightened wisdom: discriminative wisdom, mirror-like wisdom, wisdom of equality, all-accomplishing wisdom, and all-pervading wisdom.

four boundless qualities: Love, compassion, sympathetic joy, and impartiality.

garuda: (Skt.) In Indian mythology, a bird that can fly as soon as it hatches from the egg. It symbolizes self-existing, primordial wisdom.

Great Perfection: (Tib. *Dzogchen*) Also translated as the Great Completeness, it is the pinnacle of the Buddhist path to awakening, and the heart-essence of all spiritual paths. It is composed of the teachings and methods for realizing the clear and luminous nature of mind.

hope and fear: When consumed with worldly matters, we vacillate between the extremes of hope and fear. We hope that things will work out for our benefit, and we fear that they will not.

ignorance: (Tib. *ma rigpa*) The lack of knowing, a failure to recognize the empty and lucid nature of mind itself. Ignorance perceives the self and phenomena as existing substantially, independently, and self-sufficiently.

impartiality: One of the four boundless qualities. Viewing all beings equally, knowing that they wish to avoid suffering and that they desire only happiness.

indestructible nature: All phenomena arise from causes and conditions and will eventually cease to exist. Pure awareness is said to be indestructible because it does not arise from causes and conditions; therefore, it cannot be destroyed. It is beyond arising and ceasing.

interdependence: The truth that all phenomena appear based on the coming together of causes and conditions. Nothing can exist independently.

karma: (Skt.) The totality of the forces that were set in motion by previous thoughts, words, and actions. The workings of karma are not fixed; past karma can be purified, and future karma is influenced by our present thoughts and actions.

lama: (Tib.) A title in the Tibetan Buddhist tradition for a teacher who has the wisdom and capacity to guide others on the spiritual path.

liberation: See enlightenment.

Longchenpa: (Tib.) Generally considered the most brilliant scholar and adept of the Nyingma school of Tibetan Buddhism. Lived in Tibet in the fourteenth century; the *Seven Treasuries* is considered his greatest work.

love (or loving kindness): One of the four boundless qualities. The genuine wish that all beings enjoy happiness and the causes of happiness.

luminosity: Refers to the clear and knowing aspect of the mind. Phenomena are said to be luminous deities, in that everything we perceive is an expression of the mind's clarity and cognitive capacity.

mandala: (Skt.) Can literally be translated as "center and circumference." Can refer to the realm of activity of the spiritual teacher and his students.

meditation: The practice of focusing the mind, which pacifies discursive thoughts and leads to insight into the nature of mind and phenomena.

Can also refer to contemplation of spiritual teachings, such as the four boundless qualities of love, compassion, sympathetic joy, and impartiality.

merit: Positive momentum that is accumulated through virtuous actions of body, speech, and mind on the path of awakening to one's true nature.

mirror: Used as a metaphor to illustrate the empty nature of mind, which can reflect all phenomena as they are. Everything appears on the surface of a mirror, but nothing actually exists on its surface.

mirror-like wisdom: One of the five wisdoms. The impure energy of anger is transformed into mirror-like wisdom, which reflects the nature of phenomena precisely and without distortion.

mudra: (Skt.) A symbolic gesture performed with the hands as an expression of spiritual aspiration and understanding.

non-dual state: The state of pristine awareness beyond all conceptual extremes of self and other, good and bad, existence and nonexistence, and so forth.

nonmeditation: The state in which the mind is naturally aware, peaceful, and undistracted by discursive thought; therefore, in this state, the practice of formal meditation is superfluous.

obscurations: Cognitive or emotional factors that veil the pristine nature of mind. Obscurations arise due to ignorance; they are not intrinsic to the nature of mind itself.

Padmasambhava: Renowned in Tibet as the Second Buddha; the great master who brought the teachings of the Great Perfection from India to Tibet in the eighth century.

precious human birth: A human life is said to be precious because, under the right conditions, one can practice the teachings of the Buddha and attain enlightenment.

pure intention (or pure motivation): The aspiration and resolve to act for the benefit of all beings, not only for oneself.

pure perception: Perception that is free from conceptual and emotional obscurations. It is fresh and vivid in the moment, viewing all beings and phenomena purely.

realization: Occurs when obscurations are purified and one realizes the true nature of mind and phenomena.

refuge: In the Buddhist tradition, one takes refuge — or seeks protection — in the Three Jewels: the Buddha, Dharma, and Sangha.

renunciation: The resolve to follow a spiritual path due to weariness and sadness over the futility of pursuing worldly comforts and achievements.

Rinpoche: (Tib.) Literally means "precious one"; a title of respect for great Tibetan Buddhist masters.

root teacher: One's main teacher, for whom one feels the greatest rapport and devotion. The teacher who provides personal instruction and introduces one to the true nature of mind.

samsara: (Skt.) Refers to the delusion that arises from clinging to mistaken notions of "self." Self-grasping is the cause of attachment, aversion, and ignorance, which result in continuous cycles of suffering.

Sangha: (Skt.) The community of practitioners of the Buddhist path who can help to guide others.

self-liberation: The natural and spontaneous release of discursive thoughts and afflictive emotions into the open state of pure awareness.

six perfections: The practices of a bodhisattva: generosity, discipline, patience, diligence, meditation, and wisdom.

sympathetic joy: One of the four boundless qualities. Taking delight in the happiness of others and wishing that their happiness will only increase.

Three Jewels: The Buddha (teacher), the Dharma (teachings), and the Sangha (community of practitioners). A Buddhist takes refuge in the Three Jewels.

three sublime practices: (1) Generating pure intention; the wish that one's activity will benefit all beings, not just oneself. (2) Practicing that activity with attentiveness and awareness while being mindful of its ephemeral nature. (3) Dedicating the results of one's practice to the benefit of all.

true essence: Pure, primordial awareness. Our true essence is inexpressible, beyond all conceptual constructs.

true nature (or innate nature): The enlightened nature, beyond all confusion and obscurations. It is innate in all beings; therefore, all beings have the potential to become enlightened.

unconditional nature: The pure, empty nature of the mind, which reflects all phenomena but is not affected or conditioned by anything.

vajra: (Skt.) The Buddhist symbol for indestructibility and skillful means.

Vajrayana: (Skt.) The swift path that can lead to enlightenment in one lifetime. Its teachings and instructions are based on a collection of texts known as tantras.

warrior: A metaphorical term often used to describe the genuine spiritual practitioner. Practitioners courageously confront and defeat their inner obstacles and weaknesses in order to liberate themselves and benefit others.

wisdom: The pure, knowing, and luminous nature of mind, beyond all dualistic fixation.

wisdom of all-pervading space: One of the five wisdoms. Ignorance is transformed into the wisdom of all-pervading space, which is the vast and open aspect of the mind's true nature.

wisdom of equality: One of the five wisdoms. The impure energy of pride is transformed into the wisdom of equality, which views all phenomena with impartiality and equanimity.

wish-fulfilling jewel: In Indian mythology, it grants anything one could desire. It represents one's awakened nature and the capacity to fully benefit oneself and others.

INDEX

A

actions
    fine-tuning, 113–14
    habitual, 78, 93
    honesty and, 36–37
    karma and, 105–8
    reflection before, 21–22, 170
    selfish, 114
    sincerity in, 39, 40
    unkind, 21, 181
adversity, 227
altruism, 27–28
anger
    breathing with, 61
    compassion vs., 110
    conquering of, 101–2
    entrenchment of, 83
    ignorance as source of, 100
    living without, 46
    merit lost through, 171
    as negative emotion, 95, 97–98
    patience as antidote to, 97–98
    suffering caused by, 249
    universality of, 89, 161, 178
animals, compassion toward, 3
anjali mudra (respect gesture), 219–20
arrogance, 211
attachment
    in generosity, 43
    generosity as antidote to, 95–97
    living without, 46
    to loved ones, 177
    to material comforts, 251
    to relative conditions, 125, 127–28, 151–52
    to self, 91, 125–26, 166
    shattering of, 79–80
    to societal roles, 125–26, 249–50
    to thoughts/feelings, 94
awareness, 231
    breathing with, 125–26, 145
    clarity of, 241
    continuity of, 223
    fear faced with, 229
    of impermanence, 67, 155, 195–96
    of karma, 170
    moment-to-moment, 147–48
    samsara and loss of, 120
    as true human nature, 16
    wakefulness as, 53–54

B

balance, 128
beauty, 253–54
being, purpose of, 14
bias, 166, 175, 176, 234
bodhisattva, 189–90
boredom, 57
boundless qualities, four, 175–80
breath/breathing
    as ally, 101
    being present in, 53–54, 59, 101, 141–42, 146
    complete, 125–26
    confidence through, 49–50

breath/breathing (*continued*)
consciousness of, 55, 141
expending of, 56
final, 54, 55, 61, 125, 126
inseparability from, 141–42
during meditation, 138
meditation on, 144, 145–46, 179
preciousness of, 16, 39–40, 56, 59,
61–62, 251
as satisfaction, 16
universality of, 176
Buddha, 98, 117n1
human potential to become, 5, 160
human suffering witnessed by,
151–52, 176
impartiality of, 176–77
material comforts of, in early life,
156–57
as teacher, 221–22
teacher lineage traced to, 207,
209–10, 222
buddhahood, 245
buddha nature, 41, 181
Buddhism/Buddhist tradition
author's experience with, 2–5
compassion in, 25
emptiness in, 185
four boundless qualities in, 175–80
generosity in, 95–96
human life as viewed in, 49
impermanence emphasized in, 66,
69
"jail of gold" metaphor in, 129n4
karma in, 106, 113
kind heart metaphor in, 21
modern influence of, 157
practitioners of, 12
rituals of, 247
six perfections in, 169
suffering in, 13n1
Three Jewels in, 117–18, 117n1
three paths of, 97n2
three sublime practices in, 143–44

Buddhist practice
applied to daily life, 247
benefits of, 171–72, 213, 247–48
compassionate heart in, 181–83
continuous ability for, 164
without conviction, 221
experiencing worldly pleasures
before beginning, 155–57
genuine, 222
goal of, 147, 159–60, 214
during happy periods, 155
impermanence and, 245
inward looking in, 165–67
meditation in, 180
merit accumulated through,
169–72
obstacles to, 221
understanding in, 247–48
urgency of, 245
Buddhist virtues
confidence, 49–50
generosity, 43–44
honesty, 33–38
openness, 47–48
respect, 41–42
simplicity, 45–46
sincerity, 39–40

C

capitalism, 213
causality, 105
See also karma
Central Institute of Higher Tibetan
Studies (Sarnath, India), 2
change, 74, 79, 127
See also impermanence
chaos, confronting, 111–12
charity, 252
cleverness, 166
cognitive obscurations, 13n3

compassion, 3, 24, 193
    benefits of, 247–48, 251
    of the boddhisattva, 189–90
    boundless quality of, 178–79
    defined, 162
    desire transformed into, 97
    energy of, 108
    freedom through, 25
    generation of, as sublime practice, 143
    human capacity for, 29
    meaning of, 185–86
    meditation on, 179–80
    openness through, 47
    perfection of, 186
    vulnerability and birth of, 110
compassionate heart, 159–60, 181–83, 215, 243
compromise, 11–12
conditionality
    attachment to, 125, 127–28, 151–52
    changing nature of, 73–74, 152–53
    compassionate heart vs., 183, 185
    dissatisfaction caused by, 15, 53
    emptiness as freedom from, 185
    goals, pursuit of, 15
    of habits, 93
    happiness based on, 59, 187–88
    impermanence of, 161
    of love, 213
    of self, 33, 86
    suffering caused by, 188
confidence, 49–50
conflict, 89–90, 241
consumerism, 15
contentment
    mind's pure essence and, 202
    with oneself, 46
    in the present moment, 56
    as realistic goal, 161
    as success, 59
craving, 83
criticism, 41–42, 165–66

D

death
    embracing inevitability of, 65–67, 70–71, 155
    final breath at, 54, 55, 61, 125, 126
    living in the present moment and, 121
    regrets at moment of, 248
    visualizing, 61
    Western fear of, 65
    See also impermanence
dedication, 140, 143–44, 171
delusion, 202
desire
    conquering of, 101–2
    energy of, 96–97, 254
    generosity as antidote to, 95–96
    ignorance as source of, 100
    as negative emotion, 95–97
    samsara and, 109
    stimulation of, 159
    suffering caused by, 155, 249
    universality of, 161, 178
devotion, 214, 219–20, 243
Dharma, 117n1, 155, 155n1
diligence, merit accumulated through, 169
disagreement, 245–46
discipline, merit accumulated through, 169
dishonesty, 36, 37
dissatisfaction, 53, 56, 57, 59, 159, 187, 249, 254
distraction, 45, 56, 57, 142, 223
doubt, 161
dualism/duality
    freedom from, 117–18, 121, 130
    in generosity, 43–44
    source of, 89–90
dukkha ("suffering"), 13n1

E

"effortless path," the, 119–20
ego. *See* self
emotions
    conquering, 101–2, 136
    ephemeral nature of, 83
    intelligence, 23
    negative, 54, 95–100, 135, 161, 178,
      239
    obscurations, 13n3
    purification of, 97, 100
    suffering caused by, 193, 249
    universality of, 161
    validity of, 95
    See also specific emotion
emptiness, 81–82, 93–94, 119, 169–70,
   185
enemies
    bodhisattva vows not to harm, 190
    death of, 67
    internal, conquering of, 101–2
    love and, 177
    making of, 42
    meditation benefits toward, 136
energy
    of compassion, 108
    of desire, 96–97, 254
    emotions emerging from, 95
    after enlightenment, 107–8
    experience as flow of, 86
    of jealousy, 35–36
    of mind, 199–200
    of thoughts, 163, 197
    through understanding true self,
      85–86
enlightenment, 22, 23, 29, 47
    as dream, 128
    energy following attainment of,
      107–8
    human potential for, 212, 245
    living in the present moment and,
      122

    teacher and, 118
    in Vajrayana Buddhism, 97n2
envy
    conquering of, 101–2
    ignorance as source of, 100
    as negative emotion, 95, 99–100
    sympathetic joy as opposite of, 179
    universality of, 161, 178
equality, 42, 239
equanimity, 161, 201
experience, as illusion, 79–80

F

Facebook, 253
failures, 44
fame, 99
fashion, 253–54
fault-finding, 73–74, 165–66
fearlessness, 228, 230, 231, 233–35
fear(s)
    arising of, 231, 233
    confronting, 12
    constraint by, 81
    of death, 65
    ego burdened with, 200
    looking inside, 231–32
    of uncertainty, 229–30
    universality of, 161, 230
focus, during meditation, 137–40
freedom
    American view of, 9
    through compassion, 25
    embracing, 127–28
    happiness as, 252
    through living in the present
      moment, 121–22, 125, 129–30
    surrender and experience of, 9–10
friendship, 166, 245–46
frustration, 97
future, the, 59, 121, 130

G

generosity
    as antidote to desire, 95–97
    dualistic thinking and, 43–44
    happiness through, 252
    during meditation, 137
    merit accumulated through,
      169–70
gracefulness, 74
Great Perfection tradition, 3, 121–22,
    131–32, 170, 248
greed, 161, 178, 249

H

habits, 78, 91, 93, 109, 136
happiness
    being present in the breath as, 53
    Buddhist practice during, 155
    defined, 251–52
    through generosity, 252
    human striving for, 62, 180
    impermanent, 187–88
    intelligence and, 27–28
    pursuit of, 27
    understanding and, 248
    wisdom as source of, 195–96
hatred, 83
healing, 187–88
Heart Sutra, 228
"heaven," desire to reach, 227–28
hedonism, 109
Hinayana Buddhism, 97n2
honesty, 33–38, 146, 255
hope, 118, 200
human life
    brevity of, 73–74
    as dance, 243–44
    essence of, 153, 250
    misuse of, 73
    preciousness of, 49, 55–58, 62,
      70–71, 241–42, 250, 251
    purpose of, 57, 77
    taken for granted, 55–56
    wasting of, 242, 248

I

ignorance
    as affliction, 95
    afflictions arising from, 100
    conquering of, 101–2
    defined, 13n2
    dispelling of, 13
    harmful actions arising from, 181
    of impermanence, 195
    samsara as, 92
    suffering caused by, 249
illusions, shattering of, 79–80
impartiality, 175–77, 180
impermanence
    attachment shattered by, 79–80
    awareness of, 67, 155, 195–96
    Buddhist practice and, 245
    of the conditional, 161
    embracing, 65–67, 151–53
    of happiness, 187–88
    ignorance of, 195
    intellectual capacity to understand,
      14
    living nakedly in the face of, 11–12
    reflections on, 69–71, 79, 127–28,
      152–53
    of self, 86
    suffering caused by, 195
    universality of, 162
    See also death
Indian mythology, 54n1
innate nature, in Great Perfection tradi-
    tion, 131–32
innocence, 39–40
insincerity, 42

intelligence, innate
     birth of, 37
     cleverness vs., 166
     compassion and, 47
     emotional, 23
     as essence of being, 13
     happiness and, 27–28
     living in the present moment and,
          125, 250–51
     self-centered behavior abandoned
          through, 181
     universality of, 176
     utilizing, 13–14
intentions
     examining, 19, 25–26, 78
     kindhearted, 21–22, 24, 161
     purity of, 23, 25, 143
     selfish, 23
     during spiritual journey, 19–20,
          222, 227–28
     understanding others', 42
interdependence, 170, 177
Internet, 253, 254
inward looking, 165–67
iPads, 253
iPhones, 253

J

"jail of gold" metaphor, 129, 129n4
jealousy, 35–36, 46, 61, 89, 249
joy, 161, 242, 244
     in the breath, 125–26
     duality abandoned for, 121
     as expression of Buddha within, 36
     after meditation, 140
     sympathetic, 179–80
judgmentalism, 161, 165–66, 202–3

K

karma
     awareness of, 170
     good, 110

ignorance of the present moment
          and, 35
     law of, 105–8
     negative, 113, 221
     purification of, 113–14
     samsara and, 92
     suffering caused by, 193
Khenpo Karma Dorje, 3
kindheartedness
     benefits of, 247–48
     of intentions, 21–22, 24
     others deserving of, 239
     as success, 58
     of teachers, 213–15

L

living fully, 9–10, 11
     See also specific aspect
love
     boundless quality of, 177–78
     conditional, 213
     impermanence and expression of,
          66
     meditation on, 179–80
     of oneself, 85–86, 178, 241
     sincerity in, 40
luminosity, 91, 94, 119, 119n3, 220,
     222–23

M

Mahayana Buddhism, 97n2
mandala, 211–12, 211n1
material comforts, 53, 127, 146, 151–52,
     155–57, 251
meditation
     basic practice, 137–40
     benefits of, 93, 152
     on boundless qualities, 175, 179–80
     on the breath, 144, 145–46, 179
     continuous awareness as, 223
     dedication following, 140

"effortless path" and, 120
fashionability of, 152
fear confronted with, 230
honesty and, 38
merit accumulated through, 169
as necessary, 135–36
nonmeditation as, 147–48
as preparation for challenges, 228
procrastination regarding, 141
purpose of, 152–53
reinvigorating practice of, 111–12,
    151
self-supervision during, 219
site for, 148
thoughts during, 92–93
Tibetan meaning, 148
merit
    accumulation of, 169–70
    dedication of, 140, 143–44, 171–72
mind
    awareness of workings of, 197
    clear, 81–82
    compassionate nature of, 163
    energy of, 199–200
    fine-tuning, 113
    luminosity of, 91, 119n3
    as mirror, 201–3
    natural state of, 135, 148, 163–64,
        169
    pure essence of, 194, 197, 201–3
    thoughts as expressions of, 200
    wandering, 137, 223
mindfulness
    of the breath, 145, 179
    defined, 29n1
    of impermanence, 69–71, 196
    living without, 59
    of negative emotions, 99–100
    of the present moment, 35
    during spiritual journey, 29
miserliness, 106–7
mistakes, 44
moment, perfect, 119–20

moment, the. See present moment, liv-
    ing in the
monkey mind, 138
motivations. See intentions

N

negativity, 12, 61
nonattachment, 125–26, 131–32, 177
nonmeditation, as ultimate meditation,
    147–48

O

obscurations, 13n3, 81–82
openness, 37, 47–48
overindulgence, 9, 45, 109

P

Padmasambhava (Second Buddha), 3,
    170
pain, 59
past
    focus on, 42, 121
    freedom from, 130
    masters/sages of, 112
patience, 97–98, 169
perceptions, ephemeral nature of, 82–83
perfection, natural, 121–22
perfections, six, 169
pleasure-seeking, 9, 57, 59, 155–57
point of view, not clinging to, 131–32
popular culture, 57
pornography, 254
practitioners, 12
prayer, daily, 25, 214
preferences, 98, 200
present moment, living in the
    benefits of, 248
    in the breath, 53–54, 59, 101,
        141–42, 146
    cherishing, 48, 83, 188

present moment, living in the (*continued*)
    confidence in, 49–50
    defined, 252
    dualistic thinking and, 43–44
    freedom of, 125
    gracefulness in, 74
    honesty as, 34–35, 37
    as self-liberation, 129–30
    spiritual health based on, 188
    technology and, 253
    tips for, 250–51
    as true self, 121–22
    without compromise, 11–12
pride
    breathing with, 61
    conquering of, 101–2
    ignorance as source of, 100
    living without, 46
    as negative emotion, 95
    suffering caused by, 249
    universality of, 89, 161, 178
    vajra-pride, 98–99
    wisdom obstructed by, 211
procrastination, 141
progress, ideal of, 132

R

rationalizing, 37
reality
    contrived versions of, 131
    honesty as seeing, 34, 37, 146
relaxation, 152
respect
    acquisition of, 249
    as Buddhist virtue, 41–42
    equality and, 57–58
    gesture of (*anjali mudra*), 219–20
    for oneself, 241
    others deserving of, 239
    self and, 181
    for teachers, 210, 211–12, 214, 217, 242

restlessness, 159
rituals, 247

S

samsara (cycle of misery)
    awareness lost through, 120
    defined, 92
    liberation from, 109–10, 213
Sangha, 117n1
satisfaction, genuine, 15–16
self
    ambitions of, 33–34
    anger and, 98
    attachment to, 91, 125–26, 166
    conquering of, 113
    control by, 45
    deception through, 209
    discursive thoughts and, 92, 197–98
    dualistic thinking and, 43–44, 121
    energy freed from, 107–8
    exaggerated belief in, 89–90, 120
    as fearful, 202
    freedom from notion of, 81–83
    karma and, 107–8
    as mental construct, 33, 82, 195
    notion of, and profit, 83
    preferences of, 98, 200
    suffering caused by, 91
    teacher subjugation of, 209–10
    territorial, 77–78
    true, 85–86, 94, 121–22, 188
    uncertainty and, 229–30
    vulnerability of, 165–66
    weakness of, 165–66
self-centeredness, 15–16, 20, 27–28, 161, 181
self-cherishing, 23–24
self-deceit, 13–14, 37–38, 79–80, 135, 182, 209, 232
self-discipline, 10, 135, 155
self-fulfillment, 121–22

self-improvement, ideal of, 132
self-indulgence, 9, 45, 109
selfishness
    awareness of, 113–14
    consequences of, 23, 89, 161
    dishonesty and creation of, 36
    freedom from, 25
    of intentions, 21, 23, 78
    suffering caused by, 155, 186
self-liberation, 129–30, 183, 185–86
self-understanding, 182
Seven Treasures of Longchenpa, 4
sexuality, 254–55
Shyalpa Monastery and Retreat Center
    (Kham, Tibet), 3–4
Shyalpa Tenzin Rinpoche
    autobiographical sketch, 1–5
    career of, 255–56
    mother of, 156
    talk preparation by, 132
    teachers of, 207
simplicity, 5, 34, 45–46, 111, 112
sincerity, 39–40, 42, 222
smile, true, 186
social status, 45, 249
societal roles, 125–26, 131, 249–50
sorrow, 36, 242
space, 246
speech, meaningful, 239
spiritual journey
    author's experience, 2–5
    courage required for, 151
    intentions for undertaking, 19–20,
        222, 227–28
    mindfulness during, 29
    self-cherishing loosened through,
        23–24
stinginess, 106–7
stress, 147
success
    contentment as, 59
    kindheartedness as, 58
    simplicity as, 46
    worldly, 129
suffering
    Buddha's realization of, 151–52
    in Buddhist tradition, 13n1
    cause of, 91, 95, 119, 186, 188,
        193–94, 198, 200, 249
    compassion arising from, 178–79
    confronting, 222
    consciousness of, 55
    contemplation of, 155
    cycle of (see samsara)
    disappearance of, 13, 145–46, 147
    human avoidance of, 180
    ignorance of the present moment
        and, 35
    insulation from, 227
    of others, relieving, 23, 239
    universality of, 19–20
surrender, 9–10
sympathetic joy, 179–80

T

Tara (Buddhist deity), 254
teacher(s)
    author's, 207
    Buddha as, 221–22
    Buddhist lineage of, 207, 209–10,
        222
    compassionate heart of, 215, 243
    devotion to, 214, 243
    dualistic thinking and, 117–18
    as everywhere, 217
    infallible nature of, 242
    innate wisdom as, 234–35
    luminous, 222–23
    need for, 209–10, 213, 250
    respect for, 210, 211–12, 214, 217,
        219–20, 242
    unconditional kindness of, 213–15
    wisdom-mind of, 214, 215

technology, 253
television, 57
thoughts, 135
    discursive, as obscurations, 91,
        119, 179
    dissolution of, 119–20
    energy of, 163, 197
    ephemeral nature of, 82–83, 148,
        163, 164, 197
    as expressions of mind, 200
    gaps in flow of, during meditation,
        92–93, 246
    habitual, 78, 93
    independent, 91–92
    mesmerizing ability of, 137
    nature of, 197–98
    observing, 164
    selfish, 21, 114
    source of, 93
Three Jewels, 117, 117n1
Tibetan Book of the Dead, 70
Twitter, 253

U

uncertainty, 229–30
understanding, 247–48
United States
    author's relocation to, 4
    freedom as viewed in, 9
    instant-gratification society in, 4

V

vajra-pride, 99, 99n3
Vajrayana Buddhism, 97, 97n2, 207
vengeance, 61
view, profound, 233–34
vulnerability, 110, 162, 165–66

W

wakefulness, 53–54, 54n1
weaknesses
    acknowledging, 151, 159, 165–67, 189
    others' judgments of, 202–3
    universality of, 255
wealth (material), 61, 99, 249
wisdom
    all-accomplishing, 99, 100
    of all-pervading space, 100
    Buddhist qualities perfected
        through, 169–70
    through compassion, 182
    discriminative, 97, 100
    of equality, 98, 100
    happiness through, 195–96
    innate, 209, 219, 234–35
    meditation as path to, 136
    mirror-like, 98, 100
    obstructions to, 211
women, beauty of, 253–54
work, 249–50
worry, 146

About the Author

His Eminence Shyalpa Tenzin Rinpoche is a highly accomplished meditation master and learned scholar in the Tibetan Buddhist tradition. With dignity and clarity, Rinpoche uncompromisingly transmits the profound teachings of the Buddha for the benefit of all.

His fresh and authentic teaching style provides a framework for using everyday situations to realize our highest potential. With genuine compassion, he manifests in order to meet the needs of each individual. Quite simply, he is a living expression of the precious wish-fulfilling jewel of Buddhadharma. He is one of the greatest living Dzogchen masters and a perfect teacher and guide for these complex times.

Rinpoche is renowned for his sophisticated understanding of Eastern and Western cultures. His students treasure his great compassion and kindness, unyielding loyalty, sense of humor, and skill in stripping away pretense. Rinpoche enjoys an active family life with his wife and three young children.

For over twenty years, His Eminence has tirelessly given teachings, retreats, seminars, and empowerments around the world and has lectured at universities, including Harvard, Yale, and Naropa University. In 1989 Rinpoche founded Rangrig Yeshe, Inc., a nonprofit organization in the United States to preserve Vajrayana teachings. He also founded the Tibetan Children's Fund, which has educated over three hundred children in India and Nepal. In Kathmandu, Nepal, he reestablished the Shyalpa Monastery and Retreat Center, and he founded Shyalpa Nunnery. Here, Shyalpa Rinpoche guides over 130 monks and nuns in the Dzogchen Longchen Nyingtig tradition.

His Eminence Shyalpa Rinpoche is in the process of establishing the Center for Enlightenment at Buddhafield in Millerton, New York, which he calls a sanctuary for complete awareness within ourselves, in the center of our hearts. Rinpoche has also established the Dharmachakra Teaching Funds in the United States and Europe. All the revenue generated from Rinpoche's teachings goes into these funds and is used to organize and sponsor future teachings and retreats.

Rinpoche founded the nonprofit charitable organizations Wencheng Gongzhu International Foundation in Hong Kong in 2009, WGIF Taiwan in 2010, and WGIF Malaysia in 2011, in order to support his compassionate activities throughout Southeast Asia.

About Shyalpa Rinpoche's Centers and Projects

RANGRIG YESHE AND BUDDHAFIELD,
THE CENTER FOR ENLIGHTENMENT

Rangrig Yeshe, a nonprofit organization, was established in 1989 to support the compassionate activities of His Eminence Shyalpa Tenzin Rinpoche in North America. Buddhafield, the seat of Shyalpa Rinpoche in the United States, has been established in order to preserve and disseminate the profound teachings of the luminous lineage of the Great Perfection in our time and for future generations. Buddhafield, the Center for Enlightenment, is a pristine sanctuary located in Millerton, New York. For more information, please visit www.buddhafield.info.

SHYALPA MONASTERY AND NUNNERY

In 1992, Shyalpa Rinpoche reestablished the Shyalpa Monastery and Nunnery in Kopan, Kathmandu, Nepal, and in 2010 Kyunchen Mipham Shedra was instituted. In 1989, His Eminence founded the Tibetan Children's Fund. This project aids underprivileged Himalayan children living in Nepal and India, supporting their basic needs and education. For more information, please visit www.shyalparinpoche.org.

WENCHENG GONGZHU
INTERNATIONAL FOUNDATION

Shyalpa Rinpoche founded the nonprofit charitable organizations Wencheng Gongzhu International Foundation Hong Kong in 2009, WGIF Taiwan in 2010, and WGIF Malaysia in 2011 to support his compassionate activities throughout Southeast Asia. For more information, visit www.wenchenggongzhu.org.

NEW WORLD LIBRARY is dedicated to publishing books and other media that inspire and challenge us to improve the quality of our lives and the world.

We are a socially and environmentally aware company, and we strive to embody the ideals presented in our publications. We recognize that we have an ethical responsibility to our customers, our staff members, and our planet.

We serve our customers by creating the finest publications possible on personal growth, creativity, spirituality, wellness, and other areas of emerging importance. We serve New World Library employees with generous benefits, significant profit sharing, and constant encouragement to pursue their most expansive dreams.

As a member of the Green Press Initiative, we print an increasing number of books with soy-based ink on 100 percent postconsumer-waste recycled paper. Also, we power our offices with solar energy and contribute to nonprofit organizations working to make the world a better place for us all.

Our products are available
in bookstores everywhere.
For our catalog, please contact:

New World Library
14 Pamaron Way
Novato, California 94949

Phone: 415-884-2100 or 800-972-6657
Catalog requests: Ext. 50
Orders: Ext. 52
Fax: 415-884-2199
Email: escort@newworldlibrary.com

To subscribe to our electronic newsletter, visit
www.newworldlibrary.com

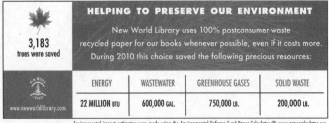

HELPING TO PRESERVE OUR ENVIRONMENT

3,183 trees were saved

New World Library uses 100% postconsumer-waste recycled paper for our books whenever possible, even if it costs more. During 2010 this choice saved the following precious resources:

www.newworldlibrary.com

ENERGY	WASTEWATER	GREENHOUSE GASES	SOLID WASTE
22 MILLION BTU	600,000 GAL.	750,000 LB.	200,000 LB.

Environmental impact estimates were made using the Environmental Defense Fund Paper Calculator @ www.papercalculator.org.